THORPE HAMLET AND THE SECOND WORLD WAR

GW00372639

Contents

Thorpe Hamlet History Group Occasional paper 4

Acknowledgments

This publication was researched and produced by members of Thorpe Hamlet History Group: Debbie Russell, Ann Shopland, Jill Halliday, Jim Marriage, Robin Bowling and John Trevelyan.

Images with 'Courtesy NCC' in the description are images from the Picture Norfolk collection (www.picture.norfolk.gov.uk) reproduced by kind permission of Norfolk County Council's Library and Information Service. Images with 'Courtesy NRO' in the description are images from, or of objects in, the collections of the Norfolk Record Office and are reproduced by kind permission of Norfolk Record Office. Other images are by History Group members or are images which are, to the best of the Group's knowledge, out of copyright or which we have permission to use.

Maps use a base of Ordnance Survey Open Data, Crown Copyright and database right 2020.

If any readers have further information about Thorpe Hamlet and the Second World War or about any of those whose sacrifice is remembered here, please contact Jim Marriage, tel 01603 436149.

First published 2020.

ISBN 978-0-9955487-3-2

Printed by Catton Print, Norwich.

Other Thorpe Hamlet History Group publications

- **A Thorpe Hamlet Miscellany**, a collection of more than 100 articles by June Marriage on behalf of the Group published in the St. Matthew's Church magazine between 2005 and 2015 (published 2016)

- **Occasional Paper 1 : Thorpe Hamlet Street Names**, (second edition, 2016)

- **Occasional Paper 2 : Shops in Thorpe Hamlet Then and Now**, (second edition, 2016)

- **Occasional Paper 3 : Thorpe Hamlet and the First World War** (2019)

The History Group has also prepared a **Thorpe Hamlet Trail.** Published by St. Matthew's Church, the Trail describes 50 places to see in Thorpe Hamlet and includes a map showing one way of linking them together.

Information about the Group can be found online at http://www.thorpehamlet.org.uk/

INTRODUCTION

A major theme of our companion volume on Thorpe Hamlet in the First World War was the sacrifice made by the men - and their families - whose loss of life is recorded on the St. Matthew's Church war memorial.

The striking contrast in the Second World War is that the war came to the population much more directly, with many air raids targeting an area of a historic city that contained a major railway station and several industrial sites and was close to a famous cathedral. At times Norwich also received evacuees from London, and this had a direct impact when Thorpe Hamlet schools had to be closed to allow evacuated children to be processed. At other times, when Norwich was itself under attack, children were evacuated away from Norwich.

As a consequence our list of those whose loss of life is commemorated in Thorpe Hamlet ranges from the elderly and very young, killed when their homes were bombed, to those who died serving in the Armed Forces in air raids over Germany, on the Normandy beaches or in Far East prisoner of war camps.

Everyday life was affected more quickly than in the First World War - not only with the actions taken by way of air raid precautions and the building of shelters -, but also with the speedier introduction of rationing.

Currency and weights and measures

Currency is expressed in pre-decimal amounts:

- 12 pence = 1 shilling
- 20 shillings = 1 pound,

thus 1 shilling was the equivalent of 5p in today's money and a penny slightly less than ½p.

It is written as £3 5s 3d (three pounds, five shillings and 3 pence) or £3/5/3. 2/8d is two shillings and eight pence.

Weights and measures are expressed in imperial measure:

- 1 oz (ounce) = approx 30g
- 1 lb (pound) (16 oz) = approx 450g
- 1 inch = approx 2.5 cm
- 1 foot (12 inches) = approx 30cm

1 : EVERYDAY LIFE

Education

With the outbreak of war schools re-opened late in 1939 after the summer holidays to enable the building of air raid shelters and prepare new timetables. Until the new shelters were completed in the playgrounds, temporary shelters were put in place in the Crome and Stuart schools in the storage space under the stages in the school halls.

As in World War I, schools lost many of their staff who joined up to fight so the female teachers who had left the profession when they married once again came back to the classroom for the duration, only to leave again when their male counterparts returned at the end of the war.

Because of lack of air raid cover a tutorial system was put in place for the pupils, this meant coming in to school for short periods and being given a supply of schoolwork to be completed at home and when done returning back to school to have work marked and to collect more. This system continued until there was sufficient space in the air raid shelters. The Education Committee ensured that children would carry on their education as normal as possible during the war years.

By January 1940 the Thorpe Hamlet schools were using a part-time system where one half of the school came to school for the morning session and the other half in the afternoon. The school hours would often change because of the blackout regulations, in the winter months the afternoon session would be from 1.30 – 3.30. There were enough places in the shelters by then for half the school to attend for one session although frequently during the colder months the shelters would get too wet for use and there would be no school until the shelters had been usable again. The Crome boys, Stuart girls and Wellesley Avenue infants school were also used as rest and feeding shelters at times of heavy bombing raids

During the heavy bombing raids on 27th and 28th April 1942 the Thorpe Hamlet primary school received serious damage and for a few weeks the pupils were having lessons in the classrooms of the Crome and Stuart schools. Eventually the site of part of the primary school was cleared and the ground the old school stood on became an ambulance depot. Later on temporary classrooms were put on the site. During the summer holidays of 1942 the headmistress of the primary school took over the Crome boys site for the holidays and arrangements for the supply of milk and meals for that period were made. After the destruction of part of the infant and junior school a large house on Cedar Road offered one

Thorpe Hamlet School after the raid. Courtesy NCC.

of its rooms to a teacher of the school (Miss Parsons) to carry on lessons on a smaller scale but on a temporary basis until the children could be accommodated in classrooms elsewhere. The local branch of the British Legion provided trestles and benches and a blackboard. Small groups of children were given half day sessions on a voluntary basis – it was not compulsory to attend.

Despite the war going on both the senior schools continued to have visits to all the factories and Gas Company, Water Board and electricity company, all with a view to future employment. There were also trips to the museums as well. The school sports event in July was a regular event, held at the C.N.S. school on Ipswich Road and run by the Norfolk Association for Athletic Sports (N.A.A.S). Swimming was later added to this event.

A regular visitor throughout the war years was the local A.R.P warden who would inspect all the gas masks and instruct pupils and staff of what to do in the event of a gas attack. The Crome boys had a visit from the local police and A.R.P warden who brought with them a selection of bombs, high explosives and incendiary devices dropped by enemy aircraft for the boys to see, luckily they were made harmless! Many children found the war years exciting and when the siren sounded for an air raid they were shepherded down to the shelters by their teachers who would read them stories or get the children singing songs for the duration until the all clear sounded. The siren was situated on the water tower just across the road on Telegraph Lane so it must have been extremely loud to the children when it started.

There were some smaller private schools in Thorpe Hamlet in the 1930s and 40s, these were fee paying and usually called "Dame schools", one of these was on Plumstead Road and was called the Ardess House School. It was run by Mrs Mabel Atthill and her daughter Kathleen, they took children between the ages of five and eleven years and charged fees of 50 shillings per term. Another school was the St. Monica's school for young ladies on Thorpe Road where the Canary Club is now, this was a bigger school but also a fee paying school.

When victory in Europe was announced on 8th May 1945 the Thorpe Hamlet schools attended for a short service of thanksgiving and then dismissed for a two day holiday as ordered by the Education Committee.

The following extracts from School Logbooks give a vivid insight into school life during the war:

Stuart School (Girls' Secondary, site now Lionwood Infant School)

The former Stuart School.

27th September 1938 "Orders received to clear 2 classrooms to accommodate 2 classes of boys from Thorpe Hamlet primary department owing to their school being used in connection with air raid precautions."

5th September 1939 "School un-able to open. (due to outbreak of war)."

5th November 1939 "School closed for afternoon for reception of evacuees."

6th November 1939 "Classes Remove, 1a, 2a and 3 dismissed as trenches were unfit for whole school."

12th November 1939 "Classes 1a and 3c absent for pm session owing to unfit trench conditions."

17th October 1941 "School closed for cleaning."

6th November 1941 "School closed for afternoon session in order for staff to a attend a lecture on 'The teaching of backward children'."

15th January 1942 "All girls dismissed at 11.00am except cookery class owing to no heat. Morning cookery to complete their practical."

26th/27th January 1942 "School dismissed for both sessions owing to lack of heating fuel."

28th April 1942 "School closed owing to raids, school used as rest and feeding centre."

30th April 1942 "School closed owing to raids, school used as rest and feeding centre."

1st May 1942 "School closed due to raids, school used as rest and feeding centre."

4th May 1942 "School commenced at 10.00am, 5 rooms being used by Thorpe Hamlet girls as their school is damaged from raids."

15th May 1942 "Primary schools returned to own school."

1st June 1942 "An extra classroom given to Mrs Thorpe making a total of 3 (a temporary arrangement)."

30th July 1942 "School closed today for mid-summer holidays, attendance very low this week owing to disturbed nights."

2nd September 1942 "School re-opened, owing to destruction of primary school by enemy action, the whole school shares the senior building with the primary girls. School operates thus;

2 classes full time; 1 class 7 sessions; 3 classes 6 sessions; 1 class 5 sessions. Staff sent out on supply by request."

23rd October 1942 "School closed for cleaning."

23rd November 1942 "Morning session only 2 classes in attendance owing to bad condition of trenches – only one trench fit for use.

Dramatic show performed by girls at Stuart School 1940.

Afternoon session primary school in attendance, only 1 class in attendance."

5th January 1943 "School opens after Christmas holiday, school still shared by primary school."

14th January 1943 "Classes 2, 2a and 1 dismissed owing to bad conditions of trenches."

13th May 1943 "33 girls selected to attend the Philharmonic concert at the Theatre Royal during the afternoon."

29th July 1943 "I Alice Sizer resign my duties as headmistress of the Stuart Senior girls school."

31st August 1943 "School re-opened, I Maud Joyce take up duties as headmistress of the Stuart Senior girls school. Miss H. M. Howell began her duties here."

18th/19th April 1945 "16 girls visited the Swan Laundry."

30th April 1945 "32 girls visited Jarrolds book binding and printing works."

3rd May 1945 "32 girls visited Lawrence and Scotts works."

8th May 1945 "School assembled in the hall at 9.00am for a service on VE day after which the girls were dismissed for the rest of the day and following day in accordance with instructions received."

10th May 1945 "School re-commenced. 32 girls visited Harmers factory."

11th June 1945 "Industrial talks for leavers at City College, 11th Nursing, 13th laundry, 18th commerce and 26th shoe manufacture."

10th September 1945 "School re-opened after summer holiday, 2 extra days having been granted as VJ holiday."

Crome School (Boys' Secondary, site now occupied by houses in Stan Petersen Close)

5th September 1939 "War with Germany declared, the schools have not re-opened and in accordance with instructions of the Director of Education joined others in the area to arrange courses of instruction in first aid and air raid precautions."

16th October 1939 "The school was opened for an emergency scheme of tutorial classes. Groups of 20 boys attended each half session to receive instruction and assignments of homework. Improvised air raid shelter has been provided in the storage well under the stage."

10th November 1939 "To meet requirements of the blackout regulations the afternoon sessions of school from today is to be from 1.30 – 3.30pm."

2nd January 1940 "School re-opened, air raid shelter for an additional 60 boys now being available. Form 3a have commenced full time instruction, other forms continue with part- time attendance."

8th January 1940 "Further air raid shelter has enabled forms 2a and 2b to begin full time instruction from today. 123 boys are in full time attendance, form 2c included in number receiving full time instruction which is now 148."

16th January 1940 "Mr D. L Drane left school to take up duty in the army."

24th January 1940 "As temperature of the classrooms at 9.00am is below 40 degrees the school was closed for the morning session. At 1.30pm fuel arrived and school was opened for the afternoon."

9th February 1940 "School closed for mid–term cleaning."

1st April 1940 "School re-opened after Easter holiday, all boys to attend full time. 230 boys from Thorpe Hamlet primary are also to be accommodated on the premises.

3rd April 1940 "Mr Killingbeck left to join the army."

15th July 1940 "As gunfire or bombs in the distance had been heard at 8.40am the boys were collected in air raid shelters as they arrived. At 10.00am registers were marked and normal work resumed."

17th July 1940 "Air raid warning 10.00am, boys taken to shelters, work resumed at 10.25am."

1st August 1940 "An air raid took place at 3.20pm, bombs were dropped within 500 yards of the school. The boys took shelter under their desks and later in the trenches. At 4.45pm boys who had not been fetched by their parents were sent home."

2nd August 1940 "School closes for 2 weeks holiday."

19th August 1940 "School re-opened. As air raid warning was given at 8.45am and all clear at 9.15am registers were marked at 10.00am. At 4.30pm a warning was given and the boys detained in the shelters until 6.00pm."

21st August 1940 "An air raid took place at 11.50am and the boys kept in shelters until the all-clear signal at 2.35pm, consequently school was closed for the afternoon session."

5th September 1940 "New school year began, admitted boys from Thorpe Hamlet, Horns Lane, George White and St. Augustine's."

2nd October 1940 "Air raid warning lasted until 12.45pm, the afternoon session began at 2.15pm."

4th October 1940 "School dismissed at 3.30pm to prepare the building to receive 1100 evacuees from London on Saturday for medical examinations and dispersal."

10th October 1940 "School closed for afternoon session to receive 500 evacuees for medical examinations."

14th October 1940 "From this date school hours will be 9.00am-12.00noon and 1.30–3.30pm."

15th October 1940 "School closed at noon for reception of London evacuees."

21st October 1940 "School closed for cleaning."

4th November 1940 "As air raid shelters were too wet to be used forms 1a and 1b were told not to attend this afternoon."

5th November 1940 "School will be closed for the afternoon to receive evacuees for distribution."

6th November 1940 "Forms 2a,2b, 2c, 1a and 1b sent home for the morning as the shelters were too wet to be used. Forms 1a and 1b attended for the afternoon. Forms 3a and 3b excluded."

9th–13th December 1940 "Owing to damp shelters and repairs being carried out each class attended for only one session each day until Friday."

20th December 1940 "School closes for Christmas holiday."

7th January 1941 "School re- opened."

24th January 1941 "Forms 3a, 2a and 1a attended in morning and forms 3b, 2b and 1b in the afternoon due to flooded shelters. Mr P.L. Fearnly left school to join the RAF."

27th January 1941 "Mrs Bullen joined the staff as a temporary teacher."

13th February 1941 "As an alert period lasted for the whole of the afternoon session no boys attended and registers were not marked."

10th March 1941 "Mr C.G. Gotts left to join the Navy."

11th March 1941 "Mrs Hill took up duties as a supply teacher."

1st May 1941 "School closed for the afternoon sessions for reception of evacuees."

22nd July 1941 "Christmas leavers examined by the school doctor."

13th January 1942 "Mr Rutherford H.M.I visited the school and observed form 3a listening to Board of Education special health broadcast for schools."

15th January 1942 "Temperature of classrooms below 40 degrees owing to lack of coke for boilers. Boys sent home at 11.50am. Full afternoon session completed."

27th January 1942 "School closed for both sessions owing to lack of heating, some rooms 32 degrees in temperature. Children whose parents were at work left in library."

28th April 1942 "As a result of a serious air raid upon the city the school was opened as a rest centre at 12.30am and functioned until 8.30pm on the 29th."

29th April 1942 "School re-opened with small attendance."

30th April 1942 "A second severe air raid necessitated opening of the rest shelter at 1.00am, this was closed at 6.30pm."

1st May 1942 "School opened as a feeding centre."

3rd May 1942 "Feeding centre closed, re-opened as rest centre."

4th May 1942 "School re-opened for children, 138 present. Revision of accommodation to admit children from Thorpe Hamlet primary girls school which was damaged in raid. Senior boys now housed in 5 rooms. Mr G. Bussey absent salvaging property from his wrecked home – returned 6/5/42 absent 2 days."

6th May 1942 "Miss Parker called with reference to use being made of school accommodation."

18th May 1942 "On the return of the Thorpe Hamlet girls school to own building, 1 room has been returned to the senior school use by Thorpe Hamlet boys."

27th June 1942 "Air raid at 2.30pm, school damaged by high explosives and incendiary bombs. Rest centre opened."

30th June 1942 "2 boys attended entrance examination at Junior Commercial school. Director and Inspector visited to arrange for accommodation of the Thorpe Hamlet primary girls school whose buildings were destroyed on 27th May."

7th July 1942 "Mr Gould – gas expert from A.R.P lectured to all scholars methods of protection, use and care of respirators."

30th July 1942 "School closed for summer holidays. Arrangements made for the supply of milk and meals during the holiday. The buildings are to be occupied by the Thorpe Hamlet girls primary school headmistress during August."

1st September 1942 "School re-opened with the temporary organisation to accommodate Thorpe Hamlet girls primary in this block. Organisation provides for full time attendance of forms 3a, 3b, 2a, 2b and 7 sessions for 1a, 1b and 6 sessions for 1c."

15th September 1942 "Miss Parker H.M.I, Mr Alsop and 2 officials of the Gas Company attended the school to see a display of the film 'It comes from coal'."

14th January 1943 "The school shelters being unfit for use all classes were sent home with instructions to return on Friday 15th."

19th March 1943 "Mr E. Clifford absent on rest centre duty at Heigham House following a raid."

17th May 1943 "Mr E. Clifford absent one week to attend A.R.P course at Southend."

2nd June 1943 "Police and wardens brought to the school a collection of bombs and explosive devices dropped by the enemy for exhibition to the children."

7th June 1943 "Mr W.V Chilvers absent owing to a case of diptheria in the family – returned 21/6/43."

11th January 1944 "School re-opens after Christmas holidays."

17th/18th January 1944 "Medical inspections for 12yr olds and summer leavers."

25th/26th/27th January 1944 "Lecturer from Gas Company gave short course to school leavers on manufacture and use of coal gas."

1st/2nd February 1944 "Lectures by representatives from the Electricity Dept."

8th/9thFebruary 1944 "Lectures to leavers from Waterworks."

22nd February 1944 "Mr Rutherford H.M.I called to inspect dining accommodation."

25th February 1944 "School closed for cleaning."

12th June 1944 "The Director of Education called with reference to the provision of kitchen accommodation for school meals."

20th June 1944 "100 boys passed through A.R.P gas vans."

16th July 1944 "School closed to be opened as a rest centre for accommodation of evacuees from Dagenham."

20th July 1944 "School re-opened."

5th September 1944 "Miss Parker H.M.I called for information concerning evacuee children admitted – 12 have been received term to date."

2nd November 1944 "A police officer gave a lecture to the school on road safety."

9th January 1945 "School re- opened after the Christmas holidays."

21st February 1945 "Mr Alsop brought Mr John Amadio (flautist) and Miss Alexander accompanist who gave a concert to the Crome and Stuart schools."

8th May 1945 "Today has been announced as 'Victory in Europe' day to celebrate the victory of the allies. 2 days of public holidays will take place. The boys assembled at 9.00am and after a short service of praise and thanksgiving were dismissed."

10th May 1945 "School re- assembled at 9.00am."

1st June 1945 "Last night a store room was broken into and the school projector was stolen."

27th July 1945 "Mr Chilvers took 30 boys to Lakenham baths in morning session for swimming tests, afternoon session devoted to school sports."

8th October 1945 "Workman began re-decorating the school."

1st November 1945 "Mrs Hill who has served on the staff since March 11th 1941 left today. Her loyal and efficient service throughout the war years has been much appreciated. Mr Gotts returned to duty on release from the army which he joined on 10th March 1941." ·

4th December 1945 "Mr R.W. Killingbeck re-joined the staff on release from the Navy."

21st December 1945 "The school closed for the Christmas holidays."

Thorpe Hamlet Primary (site now occupied by Hamlet Trust, Age UK, Ellacombe care home and a playground)

[Earlier log books were destroyed when the school was bombed in June 1942.]

1st September 1942 "School re-opened today after the summer holidays."

19th October 1942 "Owing to an alarm in operation the small number of children present remained in the shelters all morning. Only 11 children present this afternoon."

21st October 1942 "The school nurse today examined the children's heads."

23rd November 1942 "The warden arrived today to examine gas masks."

30th November 1942 "The children were medically examined this afternoon."

As it was before the bombing. Empire Day at Thorpe Hamlet School 1934.

18th December 1942 "The school closes this afternoon for Christmas and re-opens January 5th 1943."

5th January 1943 "School re-opened this morning."

21st January 1943 "Dr. Leggett visited this morning to examine class 3 there having been two cases of scarlet fever and diptheria."

27th January 1943 "The warden examined and explained gas masks today."

19th March 1943 "A raid having taken place during the night only 47 children were present this morning."

19th April 1943 "Owing to an epidemic of measles the percentage for the week is only 27.7%"

26th/27th July 1943 "Warden tested gas masks."

11th January 1944 "School re-opened after Christmas holidays. Miss Adcock and Mrs Allen commenced duties."

21st January 1944 "Medical inspections took place this morning."

2nd May 1944 "Warden inspected gas masks today."

21st September 1944 "Medical inspections and Miss Lovell from L.C.C. came to help with the evacuated children."

23rd January 1945 "Workmen came to distemper the 2 small classrooms."

20th March 1945 "Medical inspections in morning (Dr. Riddell)."

22nd March 1945 "Medical inspections in morning (Dr. Maxwell)."

28th March 1945 "School closed for Easter holiday."

4th April 1945 "School re-opened. 17 new admissions."

8th May 1945 "Two days holiday for Victory in Europe."

5th July 1945 "School closed for general election."

8th August 1945 "School closed for summer holiday until September 10th."

10th September 1945 "School re-opened. 3 days extra holiday for Victory in Japan (VJ Day)."

28th/29th October 1945 "Children aged under 5 were sent home today as there was nobody to teach them.

(no supply teachers available)."

1st November 1945 "School closed for municipal elections – polling station."

21st December 1945 "Closed for Christmas holiday this afternoon, re-open January 8th 1946."

Evacuees

As noted above, the Crome boys, Stuart girls and Wellesley Avenue infants school were also used to receive evacuee children, who had been sent out of London and other areas subject to heavy bombing raids. The evacuees would arrive at the schools where they would be given medicals and be given accommodation, many of them billeted on the newly built Plumstead Estate. The children were also given places in the local schools. The WWII display in the Museum of Norwich at the Bridewell contains a section on evacuees in Norwich and a specimen case of what the children took with them.

Evacuee's case on display at the Museum of Norwich.

Rationing

After only twenty years between the end of the First World War and the beginning of the Second World War the population of Britain again faced government restrictions, shortages and rationing. Rationing was used by the government as a means of ensuring the fair distribution of food and goods that were in short supply. As a result of continuing enemy attacks on merchant shipping carrying food and goods from overseas, many essential commodities soon became scarce or unobtainable.

Between the war years, from 1939 to 1945, the supply of nearly all foods, goods and materials was controlled by the government. As the war progressed and items became more scarce the amount of food and clothing you could buy with your coupons was reduced. By 1945 civilians were only allowed one egg a week and nearly a year's clothing coupons were needed to buy a man's overcoat. Some of the Government's most well known campaigns urged the population to 'Make do and Mend', 'Dig for Victory' and above all, avoid waste. In response to a request for an item in short supply shopkeepers would often reply 'Don't you know there's a war on?'.

Immediately after the outbreak of war on 3rd September 1939 the first commodity to be rationed was petrol on the 15th September. After registering your vehicle and collecting petrol coupons from the post office you were allowed, according to the fuel consumption of your vehicle, enough petrol to travel 1,800 miles in a stated period, which was initially a month. This basic ration for drivers could be augmented for those who had to use their vehicles for work of national importance. By 1942 petrol for private use was withdrawn completely and it was only available for work deemed essential, including emergency services, bus companies and farmers. At this time only a small percentage of the population owned cars and a great number of people, especially the less well off, cycled or walked everywhere. For those who wanted to travel longer distances there were still trains and buses. However public transport was often very overcrowded, with restricted timetables, and the government urged travellers to ask themselves 'is your journey really necessary?'.

A book of petrol coupons dated 15th September 1939.

Food

Prior to the outbreak of war in 1939 Britain imported 20,000,000 tons of food a year, which included 70% of its cheese and sugar, nearly 80% of its fruit, and 80% of all cereals and fats. The continuing enemy attacks on merchant shipping had already impacted on the supply of sugar, cereals, fruit and meat. As a result food rationing began officially on 8th January 1940 and the table below shows the standard weekly rations between 1940 and 1945.

Food rationing was introduced gradually as certain foods became scarce and in short supply. After the initial rationing of bacon, butter and sugar in January 1940, by March 1940 all meat was rationed, followed in the July by the rationing of tea and margarine. In March 1941 jam was rationed along with eggs in June and cheese in the July. By 1942 rice and dried fruit was rationed in the January, tinned tomatoes and peas in the next month and in the July sweets and chocolate. Sausages were rationed between 1942 and 1944, and people complained they contained more bread than meat.

To make sure that everyone got a fair share of the food available the government issued ration books. These books, issued by the Ministry of Food, contained dated coupons which shopkeepers cut out or crossed off when people purchased goods named on the coupons. The colour of your ration book was very important as it made sure babies, children and those with health problems were allowed any additional foods they needed. Most adults had buff coloured ration books, and pregnant women, nursing mothers and children under 5 years old, who had the first choice of fruit, a daily pint of milk and a double supply of eggs, had green books. Blue ration books were issued for children between 5 and 16 years of age as it was felt important that they had fruit, the full meat ration and half a pint of milk a day. Vegetarians were allowed an extra 3 oz (85 g) of cheese a week but meat and bacon coupons had to be surrendered. Also civilians engaged in heavy work, such as miners, railway workers and agricultural workers, received extra rations.

Meat was the only rationed item measured in cost rather than weight. One shilling and two pence, bought about 1 pound 3 ounces (540 g) of meat and until they were rationed in 1942, many people bought offal and sausages as they were cheaper than meat and they got more for their money. Whale meat and canned snoek, a type of snake mackerel, imported from South Africa were not rationed but despite this they were not a popular choice.

A number of other foods, such as dried fruit, cereals, tinned goods and biscuits were rationed using an additional points system, the number of points allocated changing according to supply and demand. Bread, potatoes, fruit and vegetables as well as fish were all 'off ration' although bread, potatoes and fish were often in short supply and subject to shortages. The 'national loaf' of wholemeal replaced the ordinary

ITEM	TYPICAL WEEKLY RATIONS 1940-1945
Eggs	1 fresh egg
Butter	2 oz (57 g)
Margarine	4 oz (113 g)
Lard	2 oz (57 g)
Cheese	1 oz (28 g). Vegetarians were allowed an extra 3 oz (85g).
Meat	1 s. 2d
Bacon and Ham	4 oz (113g)
Loose Tea	2 oz (57 g)
Sugar	8 oz (227 g)
Sweets	8 oz (227) per month
Milk	3 pints (1.7 ltrs)
Jam	2 lbs (0.91 kg) marmalade **or** 1lb (0.45 kg) jam or sugar per month **or** sugar

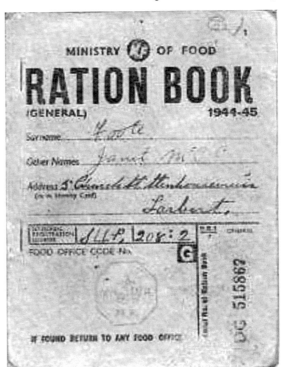

white variety and people found it mushy, grey and rather indigestible. Fish prices increased considerably and from 1941 the price of fish was controlled. As supplies of fish dropped due to enemy action long queues built up at fish mongers and fish and chip shops. Unfortunately wartime fish and chips were often of a poor standard due to the low quality fat available for frying. However fish and chips when fish was available were an 'off the ration' meal and Thorpe Hamlet had several fish and chip shops, including Albert Valori's fried fish shop 24 Bishop Bridge Road, and Lewis Pye's fried fish shop on the corner of Guelph Road and St. Leonard's Road (still open but now called Massingham's). There were also fishmongers run by Arthur Nichols at 94 Harvey Lane and William Money at 99 Quebec Road.

Every family or individual had to register with a local supplier from whom they would buy their rations. These details were then stamped into the ration book to ensure you could only purchase your rationed goods at the designated supplier. The way in which people shopped had changed very little between the first and second World Wars. Those who lived in small towns and suburbs like Thorpe Hamlet shopped locally, either at shops run by the Co-operative society in Plumstead Road and on the corner of St. Matthew's Road and Rosary Road, or mostly at small, family run shops a short walk away or on the corner of the street where they lived. This often meant that shopkeepers and their customers knew each other well, very often over a long period of time, and this kind of relationship helped many people cope with rationing and shortages.

Without fridges and the means to store fresh food people needed to shop daily for meat and other perishable foods, and as other grocery shopping could be heavy to carry, it was best to buy what you needed each day. Some of the shops may have still employed a young boy to deliver meat, fish and groceries to your home by bicycle. As well as grocery stores Thorpe Hamlet was well supplied with butchers, pork butchers, bakers, greengrocers and fishmongers. Due to rationing and shortages inevitably long queues outside shops were commonplace, especially outside greengrocers, bakeries and other shops which sold foods which were not rationed such as fish, bread, fresh vegetables and potatoes, but which were very often in short supply. Often people would reach the end of the queue to find that the shop had sold out of the item they wanted, so sometimes family members would join different queues at the same time so that if the goods ran out in one shop they may still be successful at the second one. After paper supply came under control in September 1942 paper bags and wrapping paper for most goods was prohibited and so shoppers used bags and baskets to carry their purchases home.

'Dig for Victory' and allotments

The government's highly successful 'Dig for Victory' campaign urged people to grow vegetables and fruit in their gardens, on local allotments, or indeed anywhere there was a spare piece of ground. Game and rabbit was not rationed but again they were subject to shortages and so were not always available. To supplement their meagre food rations of meat and eggs, people kept chickens, pigeons and rabbits, and the government encouraged neighbourhoods like Thorpe Hamlet to form their own pig clubs. They usually consisted of between 4 to 25 members, who were licensed by the Ministry of Food to raise pigs on kitchen and garden waste, with help sometimes from the government with foodstuffs and advice. When the pig was slaughtered, half was divided among the club members and half went to the government.

Needless to say not all pig rearing was declared to the authorities, especially in rural areas.

What is now Kett's Heights public open space in Thorpe Hamlet was in WWII land owned by the gas works. The workers cultivated crops there, and had glasshouses, but also had a pig club. The remains of the piggeries can still be seen near the pond at the top of the entrance path.

Site of the piggeries on Kett's Heights.

Restaurants and recipes

As well as growing their own vegetables and fruit, keeping chickens and rabbits, people also managed to stretch their rations by eating in what were called British Restaurants which were run by local authorities in schools and church halls. A plain three course, self-service meal cost only 9 d (equivalent to £1.72 in 2018). They were open to all and were very popular as no ration coupons were required. Also large companies based in Thorpe Hamlet, such as Boulton and Paul and Laurence Scott and Electromotors would have canteens providing lunchtime meals for their workforce. The local authority also provided school meals at schools for 4½ d a day (equivalent to 86p in 2018). Therefore a large number of the civilian population managed to supplement their rations by eating 'ration free' at their place of work, or in the case of children, at their schools. The restaurants in cities such as Norwich were initially exempt from rationing but it was soon felt that people with more money could supplement their food ration and so in May 1942 the government placed restrictions on them. They could still serve three course meals but only one dish could contain a serving of either fish, game or poultry and a low price was set for how much people could spend on a meal.

Lord Woolton, who became Minister of Food in 1940, kept food prices down through government subsides. The Ministry of Food distributed recipes to help people cope with rationing and to make the best use of the foods they had. Perhaps the most famous wartime recipe was 'Woolton Pie', which consisted of diced vegetables, such as potatoes (or parsnips), cauliflower, swede, carrots and possibly turnip, which were boiled together and then placed in a pie dish. When cool it was sprinkled with chopped parsley and covered with a crust of potato or whole-wheat pastry and baked in the oven and then served with vegetable gravy. The recipe could be adapted to reflect the availability of ingredients. By all accounts it was not well received and was, perhaps not unsurprisingly, quickly forgotten after the end of the war.

Other wartime recipes issued by The Ministry of Food

Patriotic Pudding

Ingredients
4 tablespoons of flour
4 tablespoons of grated raw potato or fine oatmeal
1 tablespoon of fat
½ tablespoon of jam
1 grated carrot
 milk and water
2 teaspoons of grated orange or lemon rind (if available)
Rub the fat into the flour. Add rest of dry ingredients and mix well. Add the jam and carrot, heated in four tablespoons of milk and mix to a soft mixture, adding more milk or water if necessary. Turn into a well greased bowl, cover and steam for an hour.

Rabbit Dumplings

Ingredients
2-3 fleshy joints of cooked rabbit
Broth they were cooked in
Scraps of bacon if possible

8 oz self-raising flour

2 oz chopped suet

Water to mix

Remove meat from joints and chop finely. Sieve flour into basin and add chopped suet, chopped meat and bacon if available. Mix with water to make a stiff paste and form into small dumplings. Boil the dumplings in the broth in a pan keeping the lid on. Serve broth and dumplings together.

Soap

By February 1942 soap was added to the list of rationed goods. All types of soap was rationed to preserve oils and fats for food. The soap ration was measured by weight, or if liquid, by quantity. By 1945 everyone was allowed four coupons a month, with babies, certain workers and invalids being given extra coupons. One coupon was needed to buy any one of the following:-

4 oz (113 g) a bar of hard soap

3 oz (85 g) a bar of toilet soap

½ oz (14 g) liquid soap

6 oz (170 g) soft soap

3 oz (85 g) soap flakes

6 oz (170 g) powdered soap

Bars of hard soap, such as Sunlight and Libby soaps, were used for household cleaning purposes, such as washing floors as well as clothes. Lever Bros. manufactured the red tablets of Lifebuoy carbolic soap, and although this was used for cleaning purposes it was also widely used as toilet soap. However Cussons actively advertised their toilet soap as not only introducing a touch of luxury to wartime austerity but more importantly, it lasted longer than other soaps and therefore helped your coupons to go further.

Clothing

Clothing rationing was announced on 1st June 1941 in response to the shortage of such materials as cotton, wool, leather and cloth, which were all needed to provide uniforms. By 1941 a quarter of the population were wearing uniforms as part of the armed forces, as well as volunteer services and organisations at home. This put enormous pressure on Britain's textile and clothing industries and so raw materials and labour was directed away from civilian production. As with food rationing, clothes rationing ensured fair shares for all with equal distribution and availability.

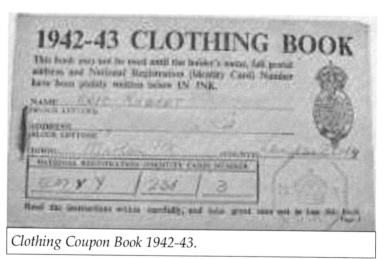

Clothing Coupon Book 1942-43.

The rationing scheme worked by allocating each type of clothing item a points value based on how much labour and material had gone into its manufacture. Everyone was issued with a pink coloured book of coupons and when buying new clothes the shopper had to hand over coupons with the correct points value. The number of points allocation shrank as the war continued. In 1941 there were 66 coupons per person per year, reduced to 48 in 1942, to 36 in 1943 and 24 in 1945. Children were issued with 10 extra points with additional coupons for older children or those classed as 'outsize'. Extra coupons were also needed for school uniforms as many schools still insisted on the wearing of uniforms. New mothers were give 50 coupons and those who needed overalls or protective clothing for work purposes were also given extra points. The tables on the next page show some examples of the number of points needed to purchase items of clothing.

In 1942 the Board of Trade introduced the Utility Clothing Scheme, and the 'CC41' utility label was a requirement on all clothing, textiles, footwear and later on furniture too. The 'CC41' logo stood for 'Controlled Commodity' and showed the item met with the government's austerity regulations. For

MEN AND BOYS	ADULT	CHILD
overcoat, mackintosh	16	7
jacket or blazer	13	8
trousers	8	6
shorts	5	3
pyjamas	8	6
pants and vests	4	2
woollen shirt	8	6
shirt other material	5	4
socks	3	1
collar, ties	1	1
scarf, gloves	2	2
boots, shoes	7	3
overalls, dungarees	6	4

WOMEN AND GIRLS	ADULT	CHILD
coats, mackintosh	14	11
jacket, short coats	11	8
woollen dress	11	8
dress other material	7	5
blouse, cardigan, jumper	5	3
apron, pinafore	3	2
nightdress	6	5
pants, corsets	3	2
petticoats, slips	4	3
pair of stockings	2	1
scarf, gloves	2	2
boots, shoes	5	3

example utility dresses could have no more than two pockets, five buttons, six seams in the skirt, two inverted or box pleats and no more than 160 inches (4 metres) of stitching and lace and frills on ladies clothing was soon banned. Ladies shoes were chunky and solid, with wedge or two inch low heels. Many women wore short skirts to save material and flat-heeled shoes together with ankle socks. It was almost impossible to buy silk or nylon stockings as these materials were needed for the manufacture of parachutes. Women were left with the choice of wearing lisle stockings or many painted their legs brown using gravy or cocoa powder, or liquid leg make-up, often 'drawing' a seam at the back with an eye brow pencil.

Clothes rationing meant that clothing became a key part of the Make Do and Mend message. People living in Thorpe Hamlet, as in the rest of the country, would have been encouraged to recycle and renovate old clothes, to use every scrap of wool or material, save buttons, and use home-made accessories, such as crocheted brooches, ribbons and braid to smarten up an outfit. Men and women's old coats were cut down to make children's coats, old jumpers and cardigans were unravelled and the wool re-knitted into a new garment. Fair isle sweaters became popular as they used up odd scraps of wool, and lacy patterned jumpers were also popular as they used less wool. This was not surprising as buying just 2 oz of new wool used one clothing point and 10 oz used eight points, equal to a pair of shoes. Clothing could be dyed or restyled and many people used furnishing fabric for dressmaking until that too was rationed. Blackout material, which was not rationed, was sometimes used to make clothes, and when obtainable parachute silk was highly prized for ladies underwear and wedding dresses. However many wartime brides just wore their best dress, a coat or a costume (a matching jacket and skirt) when they got married, or sometimes they borrowed a special dress or coat for the occasion from a relative or friend.

Although the Utility scheme offered well-designed quality and price controlled clothes it was often cheaper and used less points to buy fabric and make your own clothes. Many women were already adept at making clothes and for those who weren't the

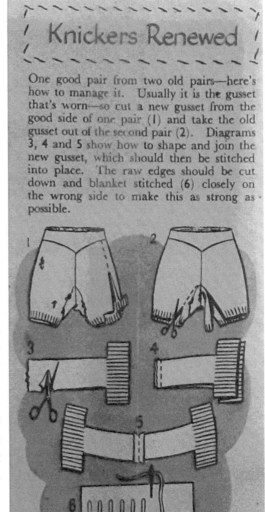

Knickers Renewed

One good pair from two old pairs—here's how to manage it. Usually it is the gusset that's worn—so cut a new gusset from the good side of one pair (1) and take the old gusset out of the second pair (2). Diagrams 3, 4 and 5 show how to shape and join the new gusset, which should then be stitched into place. The raw edges should be cut down and blanket stitched (6) closely on the wrong side to make this as strong as possible.

On display at the Museum of Norwich.

WVS, Women's Voluntary Service, held local classes in dress making and sewing, as well as clothing exchange centres. Second hand clothing was not rationed but prices were controlled so that everyone could afford to buy them.

Thorpe Hamlet was well supplied with small drapers shops, such as Miss Laddiman's drapers shop at 37 Plumstead Road, Mrs. Martin's Drapers also in Plumstead Road, Herbert Trett's drapers at 114 Rosary Road and J. & C. Tee at 56 Thorpe Road. These shops would have sold dress material, dress and knitting patterns, possibly furnishing fabrics, knitting wool, ribbon and braid, buttons and sewing aids such as needles and cottons. Most of these items were of course on ration or in very short supply and it was often an advantage if you were a regular customer at a particular shop.

Those who needed uniforms or other clothing for work were not automatically suppled with it. The Post Office Circulars record continuing discussions with the Board of Trade about the extent to which uniformed staff or other staff needing protective clothing were expected to surrender their clothing coupons in order to obtain their workwear.

Fuel

By January 1942 coal, including gas and electricity was rationed. The majority of people in Thorpe Hamlet would have used coal to heat their homes. They were allowed to buy up to 15 hundredweight (115 lbs or 50.80 kg) sacks of coal per year for domestic use. As the war progressed the population became used to frequent power cuts when all available electricity was directed towards factories engaged in war production.

Other products

Whether they were on ration or not many consumer goods became very scarce or unobtainable due to the shortages of the materials or components that were needed to produce them. These included razor blades, baby bottles, alarm clocks, frying pans and saucepans. Balloons and sugar for birthday cakes were practically impossible to find. Couples getting married used a mock cardboard and plaster wedding cake in lieu of a real tiered one, with a small cake hidden inside. Many fathers saved odd pieces of wood to build toys as birthday or Christmas presents. When cotton sheets wore thin in the middle, housewives cut them in half down the middle, and then sewed them sides to middle, and hemmed the edges. Pillow cases could be made from sound parts of discarded sheets.

The black market

There was what was known as a Black Market, in which stolen or illegally obtained food and goods that were on ration or very difficult to obtain, were sold for inflated prices. For example alcohol and cigarettes were never rationed but as they were in short supply they were often acquired on the Black Market. Goods such as these were said to have 'fallen off the back of a lorry' or were stolen from warehouses and docks. Shopkeepers sometimes kept special supplies 'behind the counter'. Despite fines of £500 and possible two year prison sentences for those involved in these illegal activities, often called 'spivs' as portrayed by Private Walker in the sitcom *Dad's Army*, the Black Market, especially in food and other rationed goods continued to thrive. By 1941 2,300 people had been prosecuted for fraud and dishonesty. However a large part of the population regarded the Black Market as unpatriotic and would have nothing to do with it.

Stationery

From as early as September 1939 newspapers were limited to 60% of their pre-war newsprint consumption and the 1942 Paper Control Order restricted their use of paper even further and by the end of the war newspapers were a quarter of their pre-war size. After the Germans occupied Norway in April 1940 Britain could no longer obtain wood pulp from Norway. Restrictions on the use of paper meant fewer books were published and schools went short of textbooks. Books were printed on poor quality paper and labelled 'War Economy'. Schools were known to whitewash sheets of newsprint for the children to have something to draw on in art lessons.

In September 1939 a Post Office Circular gave the following detailed advice on saving paper:

In view of the imperative need for diminishing the calls upon labour and shipping as well as for economy in all directions in which it is practicable, the following instructions relating to the use of paper and stationery generally should be strictly observed.

1.   A foolscap sheet should not be used when a quarto sheet would serve the purpose although a file of papers which has been started in foolscape should be continued in that size.

2.   The lighter-weight papers should, as far as possible, be used in preference to the heavier ones. For instance, the paper SS 280 should, as a rule, be used instead of SS 279 and preference should be given to the buff paper, SS 279, for all correspondence which is not likely to have to withstand much wear and tear.

3.   Typing should be done in single spacing when a machine in pica type is used but with elite type double spacing may be retained.

4.   A letter should not be written or typed on a quarto sheet when an octavo sheet is large enough. Both sides of a small sheet should be utilized in preference to only one side of a larger sheet.

5.   A new sheet of paper should not be used for a rough draft, note or message when the back of an obsolete form or even a used memorandum is available.

6.   Blotting paper should be made to serve as long as possible.

7.   Large or expensive envelopes should not be used when smaller of cheaper ones would serve. For communications within the Government service economy labels should be used wherever possible. Economy labels should always be so placed that the address is parallel to the length of the envelope.

8.   New envelopes should not be used for ordinary communication within the same office. For protection of documents old envelopes should be used or the circulation envelopes (Nos. 66, 143, and 249) which are specially designed for repeated use.

9.   Obsolete forms that are blank at the back should not be disposed of as waste paper but should be stored for issue for drafting purposes, rough notes and calculations, local records, etc.

10.   Waste paper will become valuable for making up into fresh supplies. Burning of waste paper should, therefore, be discontinued wherever arrangements can be made for its storage until there is a remunerative market for it.

After the war

Rationing did not end with the end of the war. Shortages continued and rationing of some items continued until the 1950s.

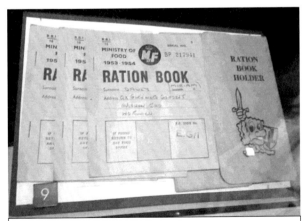

1950s ration book on display at the Museum of Norwich.

Identity cards

Another part of everyday life in World War Two, along with rationing and air-raid shelters, were identity cards. At the outbreak of war Parliament passed an emergency National Registration Bill and Royal Assent was given on 5th September 1939. This Act of Parliament set up a National Register which came into effect on National Registration Day, on 29th September 1939.

Ahead of Registration Day officials delivered forms to every household in the country which had to be completed by the 29th. The forms were collected and checked on the following Sunday and Monday and officials completed, stamped and issued identity cards to all residents. All cards at this time were the same buff/brown colour. Everyone, including children, had to carry an ID card at all times, and they had be produced on demand or presented at a police station within 24 hours.

The cards included the following information:-

- Name
- Sex
- Age
- Occupation
- Address
- Marital status
- Membership of Naval, Military or Air Force Reserves, Auxiliary Forces, Civil Defence Services.

The sections inside the card showing the any changes of address were important, as many people moved several times during the war.

On the back of the card there was the following information:-

Always carry your Identity Card. You must produce it on demand by a Police Officer in uniform or a member of HM Armed Forces in uniform on duty.

You are responsible for this Card and must not part within to any other person. You must report at once to the local National Registration Office if it is lost, destroyed, damaged or defaced.

If you find a lost Identity Card or have in your possession a Card not belonging to yourself or anyone in your charge you must hand it in at once at a Police Station or National Registration Office.

Any breach of these requirements is an offence punishable by a fine or imprisonment or both.

Obviously the main function of the ID card was identification, especially if families were separated from one another or their house was bombed and if people were killed or injured during air raids. The last census had been carried out in 1931 and so the National Register was in fact an instant census and provided accurate data on which to base planning decisions. For example the likelihood of food rationing, which was introduced in January 1940.

In 1943 the colour of ID cards was changed and class codes were used for administration and electoral purposes. Adult cards were now blue and children's cards remained buff/brown. Government officials had green ID cards with a photograph whilst those in the armed services had separate ID cards.

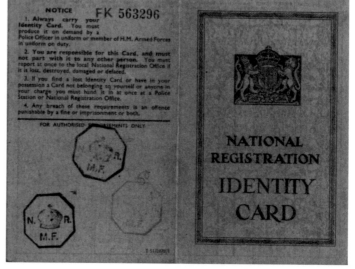

Cards were marked A, B, C, N or V.

A   Aged over 21 (adult status)

B   Aged between 16 and 21

C   Appeared on yellow cards issued to workers from Eire (Irish Free State) who were conditionally admitted to Great Britain

N   Cards reissued under an altered name (for instance on marriage)

V   Placed on yellow cards issued to people over 16 arriving in this country who declared they usually lived outside the UK.

Cards issued to children under 18 did not carry a class code.

It was not until 1952, seven years after the end of the war in 1945, that it was no longer necessary to carry an Identity Card. The National Registration Act was repealed on 22 May 1952.

Churches

With the threat of war looming and indeed the outbreak of war St. Matthew's and St. Leonard's churches were kept very busy with baptisms and marriages. From 1939 until the end of 1945 a total of 383 marriages ceremonies were performed at St. Matthew's along with 320 baptisms, St. Leonard's performed 322 baptisms – it never performed marriage ceremonies, only baptisms and funeral services.

Thorpe Hamlet for a hamlet of its size had several places of worship, these apart from St. Matthew's and St. Leonard's were the old tin church at the top of Ketts Hill (on the site of the old police house), the Jonathan Scott Memorial Hall on Thorpe Road (Methodist) and there was the original Methodist church on Ethel Road which was used as a Sunday school when the new one was opened. Both the church on Plumstead Road and the Sunday school were destroyed in bombing raids in 1942.

There were 17 Thorpe Hamlet girls who married American servicemen between 1944/45 at St. Matthew's church, along with the many other weddings and baptisms performed the vicar was kept very busy with the many funeral services performed either at the churches or at the Rosary cemetery, he certainly earned his money!

Nursing homes

There were several places to go to for nursing of all types in Thorpe Hamlet, there was the Sunnyside Nursing home on the corner of Hill House Road/ Rosary Road, this took surgical and non surgical patients. St Augustine's Lodge on St. Leonards Road was a home for unmarried mothers, Thorpe Maternity Home/Nursing home on Aspland Road, La Siesta Nursing Home run by Miss A.E Morgan A.N.H.S, this was a hostel for medical, chronic and aged cases – 212/214 Thorpe Road and also at 54 Thorpe Road was Suffolk House Nursing Home for the elderly. At the top of Ketts Hill on the corner of Britannia Road was another nursing home, all these establishments were fee paying and many closed with the start of the NHS after the war.

Football : Norwich City football club in World War II

At the beginning of World War II three games had already been played in the 1939-1940 season. The league was immediately cancelled and the results of these three games played were deleted from the records. The FA Cup started again in 1945, but league football did not start again until 1946. However during the war various regional cup competitions and friendlies were played with many players guesting for other clubs. One notable game was between Norwich City and Brighton and Hove Albion. Norwich won 18 goals to 1, their biggest win. There were mitigating circumstances. Brighton's team consisted of five of their own players, several Norwich City reserves and two soldiers recruited at the ground on the day.

Another unusual occurrence was between Norwich and Queen's Park Rangers. It was on Sunday 9th November 1941. Just before kick-off, the air-raid siren sounded. The teams waited in the dressing rooms and waited for the all-clear, but eventually the referee decided to abandon the match. Norwich played only

19 games in the 1940-1941 season. Many professionals played for Army and RAF sides while they were in the forces. The car park at Carrow Road football ground was used as a machine-gun site manned by the Home Guard. Some of the remains of the machine gun site could still be seen in the 1980's.

2 : THORPE HAMLET UNDER ATTACK

Air Raid Precautions and Civil Defence

After the First World War military experts advised that any future war would include large-scale aerial bombing of the civilian population which would result in huge casualties. In September 1935 the government set up an Air Raid Precautions committee, known as the ARP, inviting local authorities to make plans to protect their people from air raids in the event of war. These plans, known as passive air defence, included the building of air raid shelters, the evacuation of people and blackout requirements. Also the fear of gas attacks meant that nearly 40 million gas masks would be needed.

As the threat of war became closer, in April 1937 the government created an Air Raid Wardens Service which by the end of the year had recruited 200,000 volunteers, to be joined by another 500,000 by September 1938. The role of ARP wardens was open to both men and women and in May 1938 the ARP was joined by the Women's Voluntary Service. After the outbreak of war in September 1939, a small percentage of ARP wardens and members of the WVS who were full-time were paid a salary (£3 a week for men, £2 a week for women) but most volunteers were part-time and carried out their duties as well as full-time jobs. Part-time wardens were supposed to be on duty about three nights a week but this was increased during periods of heavy bombing.

The conscription of men into the armed forces meant that one in six ARP wardens were women and amongst the men a significant number of volunteers were veterans of the First World War. Although the authorities preferred wardens to be over 30 years of age, teenagers were recruited in some areas. Only men could serve in the gas contamination teams that dealt with chemical and gas bombs, the heavy rescue identified as HR and light rescue identified as LR, as well as the demolition services. The local authority was responsible for the organisation of the ARP/Civil Defence Services in their area and volunteers were assigned to different units depending on their experience and training.

As there were no significant air raids following the outbreak of war in September 1939, the main duties of the ARP wardens in the early months were to register everyone in their sector and enforce the blackout. Heavy curtains and shutters were required on all private residences, commercial premises and factories to ensure that no lights were visible which could be used by enemy bombers to locate targets. If the wardens saw a light they would often alert those responsible by shouting "Put that light out!" or "Cover that window!". Failing to observe the blackout requirements was a serious offence and persistent offenders were reported to the local police. They distributed gas masks and advised and helped with the installation of pre-fabricated air raid shelters, such as the Anderson and Morrison shelters.

ARP wardens were initially set up in temporary posts, in homes, shops and offices, and later purpose built facilities,

LIGHT IN THE DARKNESS
This ARMLET IS NOT A NOVELTY but a NECESSITY
6D IT GENUINELY LIGHTS UP 6D in the BLACK OUT
Follow instructions carefully and You will be Astonished.

On display at the Museum of Norwich.

sometimes at the junction of roads, or close to electricity, gas or water supplies as well as public air raid shelters. Each post covered a certain area and the warden was almost always a local person, as it was essential that he or she knew their area and the people living there. Each post was divided into sectors, with possibly three to six wardens in each sector, and the Wardens would patrol their sector in pairs.

On 14th May 1940 Anthony Eden asked for British men between 15 and 65 to volunteer for the Local Defence Volunteers. Over 250,000 men came forward within 24 hours, and by the end of May no fewer than 30,000 men had enrolled in Norfolk alone. Battle dress was not generally available until the end of 1940. Guns were at first in short supply, but the situation slowly improved until, by the end of 1941, all units had rifles and some ammunition. Winston Churchill did not like the name 'Defence Volunteers' and so the name was changed, on 24th July 1940, to 'Home Guard'.

Helmet worn by the Special Constabulary. On display at Time and Tide Museum, Great Yarmouth.

Although the Home Guard never had to face the enemy in battle, there were dangers and even fatalities. Terry Wasley, who had worked at Norwich Hall, was taking part in an exercise in Chapel Field Gardens and got fatally stabbed in the thigh with a bayonet. He is buried in the Rosary Cemetery, and his membership of the Home Guard is recorded on his tombstone.

ARP posts in Thorpe Hamlet

The ARP warden posts in Norwich were divided into three divisions, with separate groups within them. Thorpe was in Group C, with six posts located within Thorpe Hamlet. The ARP post C2 was based in Clarence Road, near Laurence and Scott's Gothic Works, and was the Thorpe Hamlet headquarters. The post in Cotman Road/Heathside, C6, was just round the corner from Telegraph Lane East, on the right-hand side, and there was another post, C7, on Britannia Road near St. James' Hill. Another ARP post, C4, was situated at the playground on Wolfe Road, near an air raid shelter. The C3 post on Rosary Road was near the shelters on the old football ground and behind Thompson's Tin and Metal Works. The Warden for the Rosary post lived in Beatrice Road. The post in Lion Wood Road at the corner of Plumstead Road, C5, was also near a public shelter, and like the ARP post in Cotman Road/Heathside, it was situated underground.

Apart from ensuring the blackout was observed, ARP wardens sounded air raid sirens, which in Thorpe Hamlet were sited on the Water Tower in Quebec Road. They were also responsible for guiding people into air raid shelters, evacuating areas around unexploded bombs, rescuing people where possible from properties damaged by the bombing and reporting to their control centre about incidents, fires etc. and calling in the other rescue services as required. It was essential that each Wardens' post had two-way telephone communications with the Control Centres in Sussex Street and Surrey Street, to ensure a quick response to each incident. In turn the Control Centres had direct lines to the Rescue Party depots, the Ambulance depots and the First Aid posts.

In 1941 the ARP officially changed its title to Civil Defence Service to reflect the wider range of roles it now included. Mainland Britain was divided into eleven CD regions, Norwich was based in Region 4, and services in the Eastern Region were controlled from the area headquarters in Cambridge. The Civil Defence Services included ARP wardens, Women's Voluntary Service, the Auxiliary Fire Service, (later the National Fire Service), Fire Watchers (later Fire Guard), rescue and stretcher (or first-aid) parties, the staff of control centres and messenger boys. Very often these messengers where Scouts, such as the boys who belonged to the 15th Norwich Boy Scouts based at St. Matthew's Church Hall in St. Matthew's Road. The boys cycled or acted as runners between incidents carrying information and messages to control centres and other wardens, especially when the telephones were not working..

From their formation and in the early part of the war. ARP members had no recognisable uniform but wore their own clothes and were issued with steel helmets, gas masks, arm bands and badges. The helmets had a large letter 'W' on the front to identify the wearer as an ARP warden. After October 1939 they were issued with a heavy blue cotton drill overall called a 'bluette' with a red on black ARP badge. From February 1941, all full and part-time members of the CD were issued with dark blue battledress and trousers for men and a four pocket serge tunic with skirt or trousers for women. A circular badge with the letters 'CD' topped with a king's crown , usually in yellow on a black background, was worn on the left pocket. Depending on a person's role their helmet would be marked with a letter to allow others to know what their role was at an incident:

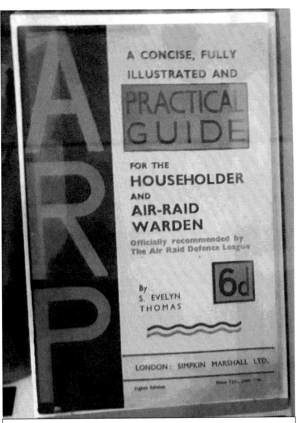

- W for wardens
- W/FG for fire guards
- R for rescue services (later HR and LR for heavy and light rescue parties.)
- FAP for first aid parties
- SP for stretcher parties (to carry injured from incidents.)
- A for ambulance drivers
- M for messenger/runner

The volunteers who were part of the CD rescue services had to attend regular training sessions, and members in

On display at the Museum of Norwich.

Thorpe Hamlet had to go to lectures in Norwich at the CD Rescue Headquarters in Sussex Street. Some of the lectures and training sessions they underwent included first aid, tunnelling in debris, shoring up buildings, rescue from damaged buildings, use of breathing apparatus and the use of derricks. There was also training for the part-time personnel who manned the CD rescue services response centres.

Few records of the Civil Defence - Rescue Services' incident reports and notes have survived but there are two brief reports and some notes in the Norwich Record Office that refer to the Baedeker Raids on Thorpe Hamlet in April/May 1942. The first report is dated 29th April 1942 and gives the 'Position of Occurrence' as Roseberry Road not Rosary Road. The mistake was quickly rectified and the address changed to Rosary Road and it was noted that the fire and rescue services were already on the scene. The ARP warden sent his request to the emergency and rescue services at Silver Road from his post near the surface air raid shelters on the former Norwich Football Ground on Rosary Road. He advised that 'HE', high explosive bombs had fallen, but no incendiary or poison gas bombs. The report does not say how many bombs had fallen as the Warden did not probably know the number at this point. Later records would show that seven 500 lb bombs had fallen on the area round the football ground, Rosary Road and Ethel Road. It records that he 'took the action' of calling out the rescue services and confirmed that there were no unexploded bombs. A Shelter Incident dated 29th April 1942 listed: "persons rescued from nearby houses numbered 14 ambulance cases, 6 sitting up cases and 5 dead (all placed in shelter). Help of first aid party and sent mortuary van." Later reports dated 30th April 1942 recorded that "two rescue parties were sent to 4 Hill House Road and one body recovered. Warden was satisfied no other casualties." Another incident report dated 30th April 1942 records that one rescue party sent to 9 Ethel Road where "3 people trapped in Morrison shelter- shelter located, no casualties found".

Although the early morning raid on Thorpe Hamlet on 1st May lasted only 45 minutes it caused massive damage resulting in many casualties and loss of life. In his 'Brief History of Cotman Road, Norwich' Neal Williams records that Cotman Road received a direct hit, and two or three 250 lb bombs fell in a line from the corner of Heathside and Cotman Roads to a point a few hundred yards from the southern walls of the Crome School. The ARP post on Cotman Road was bombed and considerable damage was done to no. 36 opposite, blowing off the roof and reducing the greenhouse to rubble.

The Civil Defence Services, including ARP wardens, were maintained throughout the war. There were still hundreds of thousands of volunteers in June 1944, although the numbers of full-time members had fallen

Public shelters and warden's posts in Thorpe Hamlet

Public shelters are indicated by black circles.
A : First aid post
S : School shelter open to the public outside school hours
W : Wardens posts
Base map OS Open Data Crown copyright and database right 2020. Shelter and warden information from maps produced by Norwich City Engineer and held in Norfolk Record Office N/EN 3/9 and N/EN 4/244.

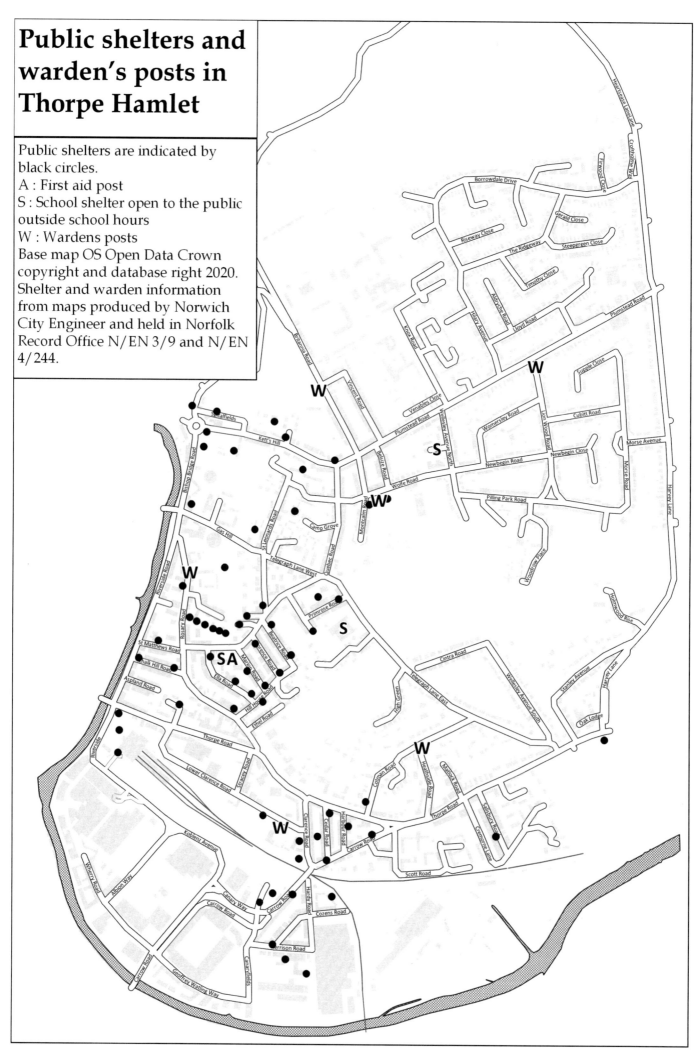

from 127,000 at the height of the Blitz, between September 1940 - May 1941, to 70,000 by the end of 1943. In all 1.4 million men and women served as ARP wardens during World War Two.

Air Raid Shelters

The site of a group of World War Two air raid shelters inside The Nest, the former Norwich City Football Ground on Rosary Road, is visible on aerial photographs taken in July 2010. A line of rectangular structures, thought to be surface air raid shelters are arranged along the southern edge of the ground. Clear paths running from these structures towards the area of housing in the south indicates they were providing protection for the local residents. Between 1942 and 1945 an additional surface shelter with a blast wall was added to the north of the site. Although in appearance this is similar to an ARP warden's post, a surface air raid shelter seems a more likely interpretation of the image given the context of the site. The ARP post was thought to be situated at the rear of Thompson's Tin & Metal Works which was next to the football ground. The chalk mines behind Thompson's were also used as air raid shelters and bunks, stretchers and toilet cubicles still remained there long after the war. Many public shelters were erected throughout Thorpe Hamlet, as shown on the map, by Norwich Corporation with financial support from the government. Shelters normally housed around 50 people. As well as the public shelters, shelters were available from the government for small groups of up to 6 people, usually families.

Anderson Shelters

These were made of corrugated iron and came in kit form with instructions and erected in gardens. They were designed in 1938 and named after Sir John Anderson. They could be used by six people at any one time and measured 2m long, 1.4 m wide and 1.8 m tall (approx. 6ft 6inches by 4ft 8 inches X 6ft tall)

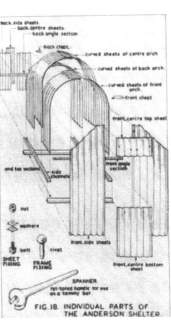

They were free to those with an income of less than £250, otherwise they cost £7. Over 1.5 million were issued. They were very effective at saving lives and preventing major injuries, but in winter they were very cold and often very damp. Because of this many people preferred to use Morrison Shelters. After the war many Anderson Shelters were dug up, taken apart and then rebuilt as garden sheds. A recreation of an Anderson shelter can be seen on the farm at Gressenhall Farm and Workhouse, although it is made of thinner metal and not buried as deeply as the real thing would have been.

Anderson shelter re-creation at Gressenhall Farm and Workhouse.

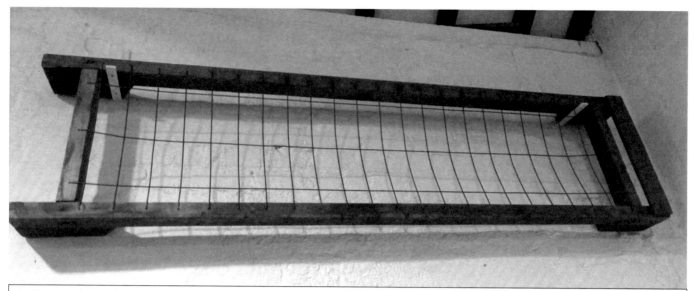

Anderson shelter bunk bed on display at Time and Tide Museum.

Morrison Shelters

These were designed by John Baker and named after the Minister of Home Security Herbert Morrison. They were shaped like a table and used inside a building at ground floor level. They were particularly effective against bomb blasts, but not designed to protect against direct hits. They were made of steel, came in kits which could be assembled at home. They were 2m long, 1.2m wide and 0.75m high (Approx. 6ft 6inches long, 4ft 6 inches wide and 2ft 6 inches high). They would be slept inside at night, and used as a table the rest of the time. Children found them good for playing ping pong on. The top was made of steel and the sides of wire mesh. Over half a million were made and given free to families who earned less than £350 a year. Although a bit of an eyesore, many people preferred them because they were much warmer in winter than Anderson shelters. A Morrison shelter can be seen in the World War displays in the Time and Tide museum in Great Yarmouth.

Morrison shelter on display at Time and Tide Museum.

Barrage Balloons

A Barrage Balloon is a large kite balloon used to defend against aircraft attack, by raising aloft cables which could cause a collision making the attacker's approach more difficult. Balloons were intended to defend against dive bombers flying at heights up to 5000 feet, forcing them to fly higher and into the range of concentrated anti-aircraft. By the middle of 1940 there were 1400 balloons, a third of them in the London area. The balloons were also partially effective against VI flying bombs, which usually flew at 2000 feet or lowe, but they did have wire cutters on their wings to counter balloons.

Known locations of Barrage Balloons in Thorpe Hamlet were:-

1. Hardy Road adjacent to Laurence & Scott. (Ref Planning Application 16/01628/NF3 dated 8th Dec 2016 for the construction of a Riverside Walk)

2. The Old Greyhound Race Track on Thorpe Road.

Air Raids on Thorpe Hamlet

The raids listed here are the ones which hit Thorpe Hamlet although during the war Norwich had a total of 44 air raids. The raid numbers are those given in the Norwich Air Raid Log Book 1940-1945 (NRO ref MC 3133/1): numbering ceases after the Baedeker raids in 1942. The Log Book also records the numbers of air raid warnings and messages received for Norwich as a whole. In total, over a period of nearly five years from 4th May 1940 to 2nd April 1945, 3513 records were made.

Bombed goods sheds at Thorpe station. Courtesy NCC, Picture Norfolk collection.

No. 1 Raid : 9th July 1940

The attack started over Mousehold hitting Barnards factory and injuring one worker and killing Harry Leonard Dye, a packer, and Arthur Shreeves, a driver. The factory site was made up of hangers and outbuildings and was hit by 12 high explosive 250kg bombs. Three unexploded bombs were then dropped. The aircraft then flew over towards the city centre reaching Carrow Works just as the workers were leaving off, several people were killed by the blast of a bomb, some were seriously injured and many suffered minor injuries. Thorpe station was next to be hit, bombs fell on the London and North Eastern Railway's locomotive sheds and hit the railway lines leaving them bent and twisted. Four bombs were dropped. Seven men were killed and a number were seriously injured. During this first raid of the war 27 Norwich people lost their lives.

9th JULY 1940

CHARLES GEORGE FREEMAN	44
BERTIE HOULT	55
STANLEY DOUGLAS LAFFLING	23
WILLIAM BENJAMIN LORD	50
RICHARD ALBERT PARKER	37
GEORGE ARTHUR PAYNE	37
ERNEST ROBERT SILOM	58

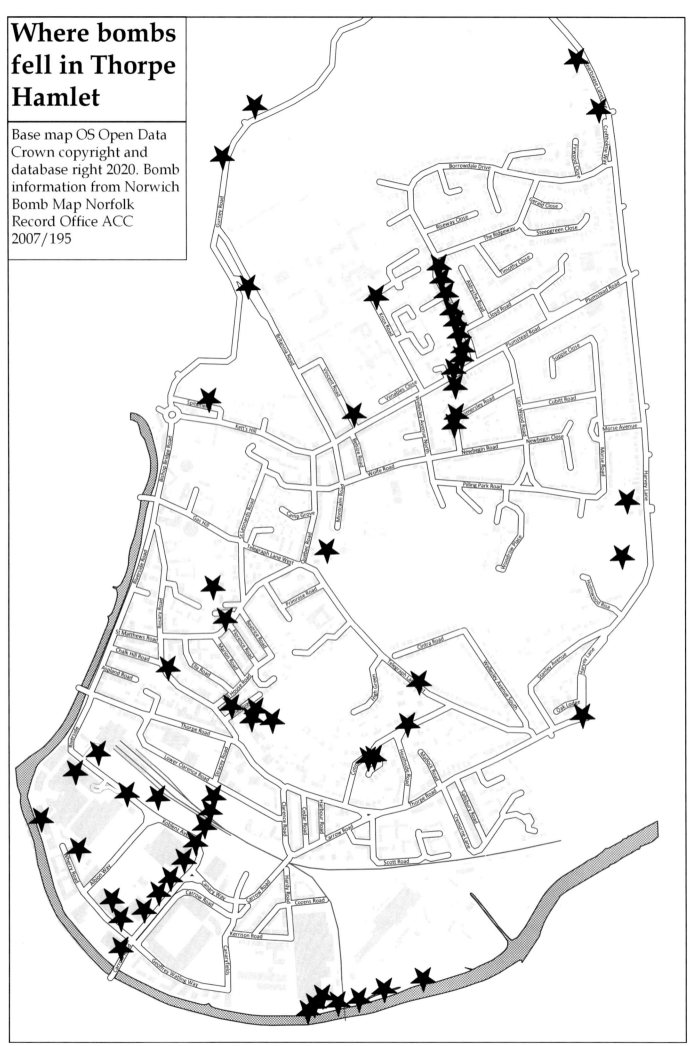

Where bombs fell in Thorpe Hamlet

Base map OS Open Data Crown copyright and database right 2020. Bomb information from Norwich Bomb Map Norfolk Record Office ACC 2007/195

No. 4 Raid : 1st August 1940

Boulton and Paul's was hit again as employees in the staff canteen did not hear the approach of the Junkers 88 bomber swooping down to 400ft to drop bombs which landed on the paint shop. It was built in 1916 of wood and the outside was heavily ornamented with mouldings and was well stocked with varnishes and spirits – a perfect fuel for a fire. It was hit by two high explosive and two incendiary bombs and exploded in a sheet of fire. Nine people died – three women from the canteen, three more from the printing and stationery office, two men from the drawing office and another from the joinery. Thorpe station was next to be hit. Although only two bombs fell and one failed to explode, four men were killed.

No. 6 Raid : 20th August 1940

At about 3.00am during the all clear period, incendiary bombs were dropped falling at random. 24 Supple Close, off Lion Wood Road, received an incendiary in its backyard some 20ft from the house. (Incendiary bombs were best dealt with by throwing a sandbag over them and thoroughly soaked with the use of a stirrup pump and bucket of water.)

No. 8 Raid : 18th/19th September 1940

Just four bombs dropped in this raid, two incendiary oil bombs and two delayed-action high-explosive bombs. They fell 55 minutes after midnight, one of the delayed action bombs fell on heathland at Long Valley, Mousehold and exploded 12 hours later while the two incendiaries which also fell at Mousehold caused minor fires to the heathland. The other high explosive was dropped on Theatre Street. During this month the air raid siren sounded 129 times with not a single day without an alert.

No. 9 Raid : 27th October 1940

Bombs were dropped on Mousehold, at the corner of Valley Drive and Heartsease Lane, and near the Memorial Cottages.

No. 11 Raid : 11th November 1940 04.05hrs

Only incendiary bombs were dropped in this raid and a majority of these landed in gardens and on roadways. The fire brigade was called to put out small fires at 45 Vincent Road and 55 Britannia Road. It was thought that this was the only raid carried out by an Italian aircraft. Bombs were recorded in Britannia Road, Pilling Park Road, Matlock Road, Vincent Road and Quebec Road.

No. 16 Raid : 4th February 1941 23.19hrs

High explosive bombs were dropped on two houses and bungalows and blast damaged several properties. Mrs Brown and her mother of 58 Womersley Road had a remarkable escape, both ladies were sitting in a downstairs room knitting when the ceiling collapsed. Fortunately the joists and the ceiling tilted forwards intact leaving a cavity where the ladies were sitting and apart from a cut to Mrs Brown's head they escaped unhurt .Another bomb fell between 60 and 62 Womersley Road and blast caused damage to windows and doors. In Plumstead

Bombed house in Womersley Road. Courtesy NCC.

Boulton and Paul's Riverside works after a bombing raid. Courtesy NCC, Picture Norfolk collection.

Road number 104 was completely demolished and two bungalows, numbers 91 and 93, were also destroyed. Seven bombs hit Hilary Avenue – six of these landing on roads and gardens. Those on the road damaged water mains but apart from broken windows very little other damage was done. Seven more bombs fell across Edwards Quarry and Valley Drive, all making craters some six feet in diameter. Boulton and Paul's despatch department also suffered some damage. During this raid seven people were injured – two fatally.

No. 21 Raid : 2nd April 1941 14.22 hrs

A minute after the second alert sounded a Dornier 215 approached in a shallow dive. Two large high-explosive bombs were dropped. One fell at Thorpe Station hitting numbers 1 and 2 goods yards damaging several trucks and causing one fatality. The other one fell close by on waste ground causing no damage.

No. 22 Raid : 8th April 1941

Incendiary bombs were recorded at Thorpe station.

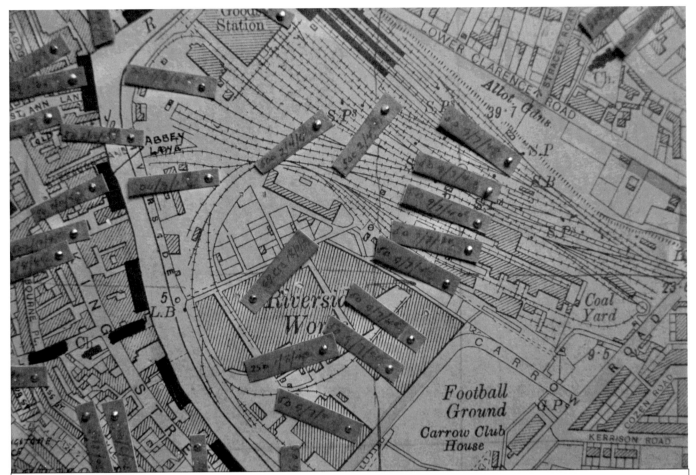

Detail from the Norwich Bomb Map showing location of attacks on Riverside. Courtesy NRO ACC 2007/195 Norwich Bomb Map detail 049.

No. 23 Raid : 29th April 1941 21.55 hrs

A warm spring evening and at 10.00pm, five minutes after the alert sounded the factory sirens gave the warning. Seven minutes later major fires and a great deal of damage was caused by a high explosive and incendiary bombs. Incendiaries fell on Laurence and Scott Electromotors, Boulton and Paul's and houses on the adjoining Hardy Road and Cozens Road, all were immediately extinguished.

No. 26 Raid : 10th May 1941

Bombs were recorded at Laurence & Scott on Thorpe Road.

Baedeker raids : 27th April - 1st May 1942

Between 27th April and 1st May 1st 1942 Norwich, Exeter, Bath, York and Canterbury were subjected to heavy bombing raids. These raids were part of what became known as the Baedeker Raids, named after entries in the Baedeker Guidebook which pinpointed these cities as historic, cultural centres. The raids were seen as reprisals for the bombing of the historic German city of Lübeck on 28th March 1942. The bombing raids caused widespread and considerable damage to Norwich city centre and the surrounding districts like Thorpe Hamlet.

However the majority of the historic buildings in the city escaped serious damage as the raiders concentrated more on the residential areas. Casualties were heavy: 162 people were killed, including fire watchers, ambulance men and a member of the Home Guard, and over 400 people were injured.

In the book 'Betty's Wartime Diary, 1939-1945, part II' the author recorded in her diary on 29th April: "It's so terrible to see what has happened to Norwich. I don't know what to say after seeing such sights. So many people not knowing what to do, and only wanting the simplest of things like a change of clothes and being able to make a cup of tea whenever you want. I think it will take a long while before some of them are back to normal again."

- Cotman Road – Received a direct hit, two or three bombs intended for Laurence and Scott's fell in a line from the corner of Heathside Road and Cotman Road. The ARP post on the corner of Cotman Road received a direct hit, number 36 Cotman Road received serious damage blowing the roof off, number 42 received a direct hit and was completely destroyed killing Mrs Blomefield and her companion. (Laurence and Scott were storing their valuable papers in this property for safe keeping.) Number 40 was so badly damaged it had to be demolished, and number 32 was set alight by a fire bomb – the house was gutted leaving just the walls standing.
- Ethel Road/Hill House Road – A 500kg bomb destroyed four houses.
- Ella Road – A 500kg bomb scored a direct hit on one house and blast damaged 13 other properties.
- Rosary Road - The Goodyear Tyre Depot, the Kings Arms PH, Robinsons Garage, the Evening Gun PH, the Norwich Gas Social Club, buildings of the old football ground (the Nest), the superintendent's house at the Rosary Cemetery and St. Matthews church all sustained varying degrees of damage.
- St. Leonards Road - Bombs destroyed five houses and damaged Thorpe Hamlet school and many other properties including the Raven's grocery store killing Cyril Raven and his two daughters Zena and Patricia.

27th June 1942 02.05 hrs

A full moon shone down on Norwich to aid the enemy aircraft with their bombing raid. An estimated 33 high explosives and 20,000 incendiaries were dropped onto the city.

- Cotman Road - number 16 demolished (250kg bomb)
- Harvey Lane – three houses past Morrison Lodge PH badly damaged.
- Knox Road – prison 250kg bomb direct hit on prison wall.
- Mousehold – near Barracks 250kg bomb – crater
- Quebec Road – 250kg bomb in Waterworks – crater.
- Rosary Road – Cemetery – 250kg bomb – lodge demolished.
- Spitalfields – numbers 39/41 250kg bomb – two houses demolished.
- Telegraph Lane (Hillcrest) – 250kg bomb – large crater in road.
- Thorpe Road – Thorpe Station – goods yard – 250kg bomb – damage to goods shed.
- Vincent Road – numbers 4 and 6 – 250kg bomb – two houses demolished and five fatalities.

Incendiary damage to following roads –
- Camp Road – damage to properties.
- Carrow Road – Norwich City Football Ground.
- Lloyd Road, Marion Road, Pilling Park Road (in woods)
- Plumstead Road numbers 29 and 74 and top of Ketts Hill.
- St. Leonards Road – Thorpe Hamlet school.
- St. Matthews Road.
- Thorpe Road – Thorpe Station goods department and Red Cross Hut.
- Vincent Road and Wellesley Avenue – number 1.

5th December 1942 12.43hrs

Anti aircraft guns roared into action as a Dornier 217 approached the city, the pilot shaken by this attack narrowly missed the cable of a barrage balloon at Thorpe. The pilot jettisoned his bombs and a stick of 4 500kg high explosives which fell 150 yards south of a gun site straddling Heartsease Lane. These bombs were delayed action and were removed on Tuesday 8th by the bomb disposal squad.

1st January 1943

Bombs were recorded on Mousehold Heath, behind the Pavilion.

18th March 1943

Bombs were recorded at Trowse Swing Bridge.

War Time Assistance Board

Anyone injured as a result of enemy action received help from the Assistance Board where immediate grants could be obtained by injured people who had temporarily lost their earning power. A married man was allowed £1 5s a week while in hospital and £1 13s weekly when he came out and in addition was able to claim 4s a week for each of his first two children and 3s a week for any other children.

An unmarried man could claim 11s per week while in hospital and £1 per week while convalescent. The rates for a single woman was 9s 6d a week while in hospital and 18s a week while convalescent.

3 : RECOLLECTIONS

By Jim Marriage

How Hitler did me a favour

I was six years old when the war started. We had just moved house, and shortly after, when I was seven years old, I was transferred from an infants' school to a junior school. Good teachers were hard to come by and unfortunately mine was one of the worst. Admittedly I was a bit slow, not wanting to give an answer unless I was sure it was right. The teacher's only answer to this was heavy sarcasm, and if this did not have any effect he resorted to hitting me very, very hard. Consequently I started to play truant. My mother found out of course as I had been seen wandering around the town common, when I should have been at school. My mother came to the school, marched into the classroom and set about the teacher. June, much later to become my wife, was in the same class, although I did not know it at the time, remembered all this quite clearly. The whole business was settled very satisfactorily from my point of view, although most people would not see it that way. Our house was destroyed by incendiary bombs; we were in the cellar at the time and all escaped unhurt. We had to move to a different district. My new school was much nicer and I had a wonderful sympathetic woman teacher. Thank you Mr Hitler.

The young Jim Marriage.

How daft can you get?

I was still at a Grammar School, aged 11, when the war ended. The School's history dated back to the 1400's, and had long established traditions, one of which was that all the teachers had to be male. During World War II this had become a problem and several female teachers had to be employed. But the school wasn't going to give in completely, so a compromise had to be made. This was that if a student (It was a boys' school) addressed a woman teacher he had to call her 'Sir'. What a daft idea, but it's amazing how quickly you get used to it. The only time it became embarrassing was if you visited another school with female teachers and you addressed them as 'Sir', the students found it hilarious.

By Debbie Russell

Camp Road

My grandparents lived on Camp Road and were fortunate enough to have the largest garden on the road as the house was an end plot, it also didn't have a split rear garden so the growing space my grandad had was a fair size. My mum was 4yrs old and my aunt 5yrs when the war started and they both went to the Thorpe Hamlet school on St. Leonards Road, they both remember only going to school for half days and feeling jealous when the other was at home. My aunt remembers being taken down to the shelters in the playground during the alarm sounding and being read stories.

My grandparents house was three bedroomed, it had a middle room and front room (which was only used at Christmas or unless somebody was really ill) and a kitchen with a fireplace , a sink with just a cold tap and no bathroom, every week the tin bath would be brought in from the wash house up the garden and everyone would bathe in front of the fire then it was emptied out and taken back to the washhouse until the following week. My nan had to do the weekly wash in the wash house which had a boiler with a space under it to light a fire, after the clothes had had a boil they were then rinsed in the large stone sink and put through the mangle to get the water out. The toilet was outside next to the wash house and was lit in the winter by a tilley lamp otherwise you just had to keep the door open, it was always cold whatever the season!

Grandad liked to grow things, in his garden he had fruit trees (apples both eating and cooking) pears, plums, he grew raspberries, redcurrants, gooseberries, rhubarb, potatoes, carrots, onions, cabbages, sprouts and beetroot. He also kept chickens and rabbits and pigeons at the top of the garden as well.

Grandad and his dad and brothers kept pigs over Mousehold as well and provided some of the local butchers with pork. My mum and aunt always say that they never went hungry during the war and never felt that they went without anything. They remember wearing their day clothes to bed sometimes to save time when the siren went during the night, and nan used to have a basket by the back door with food and drink and hot water bottles ready. Their Anderson shelter was only a few feet from the house and it had small beds in for the girls to sleep in. Many years later when my uncles were young they used the old shelter as a den and as children me and my brother used to play in it, it was still intact up to the day the house was demolished for the slum clearance.

Debbie's mum and aunt, Beryl and Jean Copland, in 1940.

During a raid one night an incendiary bomb landed in my grandad's compost heap but failed to go off which was a good thing as it was only a few feet from the shelter! Grandad was an ARP warden and when the siren went off he would make sure my nan and mum and aunt were in the shelter, then he would go to the other end house in the row to make sure my great grandparents had got to their shelter although my great grandfather often refused to get out of bed saying if it was his time to go then he'll go in his own bed! The Germans never did get him he died many years later!

When peace was declared my mum and aunt remembers being taken to a pub on Barrack Street with nan and grandad called the Marquis of Granby and a party was held there and everyone was in the street singing 'When the lights go on again'. Not long afterwards grandad who worked for Colman's was sent to London to help with street building and he was there for nearly 5 years.

By Don Cullum

I lived in Bishopgate and in 1941 attended Thorpe Hamlet Infants school. I have a feeling the head was Miss Brittain. Walking to school meant crossing Bishop Bridge and my nose firmly held, running past Ramsays the stinking hide dressers. That old wooden building looked very ramshackle even then. I came to look forward to air raids because this meant we would be read Brer Rabbit stories by Miss Castleton — I seem to remember her being a young attractive woman. I don't think it occurred to any of us kids that there was any danger from the air raids as we were safely ensconced in the shelter. Going home from school one day a friend and I were quickly ushered by a neighbour, Mr Sydney Groom into a large chalk cavern on Rosary Road, this again was due to an air raid.

By Douglas Scales

I was 8yrs old when the 2nd World War broke out. During the early part of the war I attended Thorpe Hamlet Junior school, the teacher of our class was Miss Smith, now Miss Smith was very very strict and we were all scared of her. For some reason just before Christmas, Miss Smith had one of us boys out at the front of the class. I can remember his surname but we'll call him Brown. Miss Smith said to him 'Good King Wenceslas looked out, the next line Brown?" After about the fourth time a trembling Brown replied "In his pink pyjamas", this brought forth a spontaneous burst of laughter from the rest of the class at which Miss Smith became very angry. But I was witness to another event which I can still picture today which seemed to say that there was another side to Miss Smith. During one playtime we were all enjoying ourselves in the playground when without warning an enemy plane dived out of the sky with its guns blazing, fortunately not in our direction. There was a rush for the two entrances to the shelter, making for one of the entrances I noticed Miss Smith at the other entrance, arms outstretched like a mother hen herding a group of children into the shelter. You know I think she thought the world of us looking back.

By Pauline Scales

In September 1939 the schools closed while trenches were dug for shelters. This happened throughout the city. I started at the Blyth School where we spent an hour a week copying out the work we had to do at home and hand it in the following week. Younger children had an extended holiday. I always walked to school — as did many others — until I acquired a bicycle. My father was an air raid warden as was Patience Harbord who lived in Mousehold House, their post was on the corner of Lionwood Road and Plumstead Road. I remember enjoying an exercise when they arranged 'incidents' at various points. As each incident was marked by a firework (pre war supplies), we accompanied our father on his round offering willing hands to hold the sparklers. We lived on Wellesley Avenue and during one raid in 1942 number 1 was hit by an incendiary bomb but was extinguished, damaged being confined to the roof. About 4 houses were destroyed in Womersley Close and bungalows either side of Plumstead Road adjacent. The shop owned by Mr Laddiman which was a drapers was also destroyed as was Raven's shop down near the middle school. Also on the 27th April 1942 the flares and burning barrage balloons lit up the sky. On the 29th the raid was shorter as anti-aircraft guns had been returned to us from Gt. Yarmouth — sent there for a visit from the king. It was noisier too, we could hear the orders of one gun crew, I believe it was at the top of the road. A favourite walk on a Sunday was to the old airfield off Heartsease Lane. During the war it was used by the army for anti- aircraft guns, the sort with multiple barrels. Houses had their own air-raid shelters, either Morrison or Anderson, we had an Anderson and at the time when there were regular raids that is where we slept. My father built bunks and made a barricade of sandbags by the entrance. My mother and Mrs Larke spent hours cutting out winceyette pyjamas for the troops. Bales of cloth were delivered by Lady Mayhew and the pair were famed by their ability to get more pyjamas than expected from each bale. They were allowed to keep any small pieces from which they made us patchwork pyjamas.

From 'Voices of Thorpe Hamlet'

In 2011 the Norwich Living History Group came to Thorpe Hamlet and recorded the memories of a number of local residents. Extracts from those relating to World War II are reproduced below. The History Group is grateful to the interviewees and their families for permission to use these memories. INT means one of the interviewers from the Living History Group.

Brian Hickling

INT : You would have been about five or six when the Blitz was on. Do you remember it?

BH : Yes, I do. We had an Anderson shelter in the back garden and the neighbours had shelters in tandem so all the families went down at night. The neighbour was an ARP warden and he would come back and say "They're getting it bad in Norwich tonight". Every morning my mother would open the curtains and she's see the top of the Cathedral spire and her words, always the same, "the Cathedral's still there", every morning during the Blitz it was like that.

INT : How did you feel as a child? Did it affect you?

BH : The first bombing raid we didn't get to the shelters, we finished up in a cupboard under the stairs, soot came down the chimney, the blackout fell off the window and we had two broken windows and I was quite frightened. But after that for children it was a bit of an adventure, I think. A boy could tell what the plane was from the engine sound – I couldn't now but I could then 0 Spitfires, whatever, it was quite exciting but frightening.

Beryl Vickers

BV: I remember going to the little Thorpe Hamlet School which was on Ella Road and during the war it got bombed and when I was 12 I went to the Mod on Dereham Road.

INT: What do you remember of your time in Ella Road? How many children were in your class?

BV: Not really many we never had a lot of children in the class and we had some lovely teachers they were really nice in those days and then we always used to have May Day, always had maypoles and a

Queen of the May. Never a day off.

INT: Was there a big playground?

BV: No, not very big, it was where the playground and the old people's home are now. There was more of the school on the top road and the main entrance was on St Leonard's Road.

INT: What sort of games did you play?

BV: We used to play hoopla, skipping ropes a lot and Five Stones, hopscotch and balls against the wall. There used to be an awful lot of little shops around here. One sweet shop was on the corner of St Leonard's Road and some girls who went to school with me lived there and during the war that got bombed and two of the girls were killed. I always remember going in the sweet shop there because I used to buy these teeny weeny floral gums, tiny gums all perfumed and i used to get a bag full for a halfpenny.

INT: You got bombed quite close then in this area?

BV: Oh yes there was the gas holder in front here and that was hit with an incendiary bomb and that blew up and the flames went miles high, you can imagine the gas in the holder. We had variegated ivy all along the front of the house then and the heat burnt all the ivy and blistered all the paint. We were down the air raid shelter, which we've still got in the garden. One time a plane went over and machine-gunned the top of a holder and my dad and another man went out and threw sandbags over the holes that the bullets had made and they never thought that the whole lot could go up. When we had the blitz the whole of the city was alight. Most of the people living round here used to go to Chalk Hill Works because they had an air raid shelter in the chalk hill. Nearly everybody used to go there and we'd be the only family that didn't, we went in our shelter. My mum wouldn't go she said you'd never know what diseases you might catch.

INT: Did your mother have any problem with getting supplies?

BV: No we were pretty lucky because my gran had a couple of grocery shops, one in Fishergate and one in St Johns Street, and people would often not want their butter as they'd rather have margarine so the butter that was left over came to us. At the gas works they had the pig club and they had piggeries up where the Heights is now and there was about ten of them, they each had a share. All the food that was left over from different places like Curl's and Bunting's, they'd give to the works and they'd feed it to the pigs. Every so often when they had a pig that was ready for slaughtering, I think you had to give two to the government and then one you kept yourself and then all the men in the pig club had a share of a pig, so often you had real fresh pork, which was lovely. Over on part of our garden we had vegetables and chickens and an orchard.

4 : THE ARMED FORCES AND THEIR SUPPORT

Iron for the war effort

The Cooper Mausoleum and its railings, Rosary Cemetery.

In 1942 Lord Beaverbrook proposed that iron railings and gates throughout the country should be removed to help the war effort. In the Rosary Cemetery the Trustees agreed in August 1940 that they would permit the removal of railings subject to the approval of the plot owners. Some did agree including the Colman family, but the Galsworthy family refused to permit the removal of the railings around the Cooper Mausoleum.

While the removal of the iron railings and gates is recounted by hundreds of eye witnesses, there are no similar reports of iron arriving at the steelworks to be loaded into the blast furnaces. One theory is that far more iron was collected than was needed or could be processed. Faced with an oversupply, rather than halt the collection, which had been a unifying effort for the country and of great propaganda value, the government allowed it to continue. The ironwork collected was stockpiled away from public view. After the war it has been suggested that the government did not want to reveal that the sacrifice of so much highly valued ironwork had been in vain, and so it was quietly disposed of. Only 26% of the ironwork collected was used for munitions.

The Women's Voluntary Service (WVS)

One of the largest and probably most well known of the civilian volunteer groups during World War Two was the Women's Voluntary Service. It became known as the WVS and it was set up in 1938 as part of the Air Raid Precaution services (ARP) and Lady Stella Reading was asked to set it up as a women's organisation which would help in possible air attacks in the event of war. When war broke out in September 1939 the WVS already had 165,000 members, and as their work quickly diversified into helping in all areas of the Home Front they were renamed the Women's Voluntary Service for Civil Defence in February 1941. By this time the WVS had enrolled its millionth member.

Many were older women as younger women were called up into the services or were engaged in essential war work. As volunteers they often combined working part-time for the WVS with looking after their homes and families. Apart from a small administrative staff, WVS members were unpaid and had to buy their own uniforms, using their own clothing coupons. Their dark green coats and dresses with burgundy coloured cardigans, green and burgundy scarves and felt hats became a familiar sight in the war years.

The WVS centre in Norwich was one of almost 2.000 set up around Britain during 1939 -1945. In 1941 alone 25 of these centres were destroyed by enemy action and by the end of the war 243 members had lost their lives.

One of their earliest tasks was to assist with the evacuation and billeting of mothers and children away from large cities to the country, and areas like Thorpe Hamlet, away from the bombing. The local schools, such as the Crome Boys' School and the Stuart Girls' School in Telegraph Lane West, as well as Wellesley Infants' School were used by the WVS as reception centres for evacuees. They not only used local schools, but church halls including St. Matthew's Church Hall, on St. Matthew's Road, the Jonathan Scott Methodist Church Hall on Thorpe Road and a hall on Ethel Road. The WVS used these premises as rest centres because they had catering equipment, toilets, washing facilities and space to offer temporary accommodation to those whose homes had been destroyed. As well as providing clothing and shelter to the homeless they also ran mobile canteens for the ambulance crews, firemen and rescue workers at incident scenes. Often those setting up mobile canteens were in danger from fires, fractured gas mains and falling buildings.

The volunteers were often responsible for the of running salvage drives to generate raw materials for the war effort, which included collecting aluminium saucepans and kitchen utensils and the removal of iron railings from public buildings, parks and houses.

They were involved in nearly every aspect of wartime life. The WVS collected and organised clothing for those in need, ran exchange centres where babies and children's clothes could be exchanged for larger sizes, held classes in dress-making knitting and First Aid. Members staffed hostels, and helped to run the government backed 'British Restaurants' where basic meals were sold at reasonable prices, off-ration. The WVS volunteers helped to keep the price of the meals down by helping with the catering, cooking and washing up.

When American troops began to arrive in Britain in 1942 the WVS ran 'British Welcome Clubs' in an attempt to bridge the gap between the troops and British civilians. Later in the war they took on another role, staffing Incident Inquiry Points to give information to relatives and friends about those killed or injured in the bombing.

At the end of the war the Home Office announced that the WVS would continue for possibly two years. In fact the WVS continues to this day, providing support in emergences and carrying out welfare services. In 1966 the organisation was awarded royal status and became the Women's Royal Voluntary Service (WRVS).

The Americans in Thorpe Hamlet

During the war many American forces, especially airmen, were stationed in Norfolk. Although none are known to have been based in Thorpe Hamlet, the American Air Force used Carrow Road football ground on at least two occasions to put on a Rodeo to raise money for charity. Images and other information can be seen on the website of the Second Air Division Memorial Library (see 'Sources').

Events included :-

- Steer Riding.

- Bucking Horses.

- Bare Back Relays.

- Catch the "Greasy Pig" competition.

- Yodelling by Montana Slim aka Sgt Gene Radcliffe.

- A Hill Billy Band.

Mousehold Heath Prisoner of War Camp

Over 400,000 German, Italian, Ukrainian and other prisoners of war came to the UK between 1939 and 1948. There were over 1,000 prisoner of war camps. Many have disappeared without trace and their localities are unknown, but English Heritage have managed to list 1026. One of them was on Mousehold Heath situated between the present Pitch and Putt Course and Mousehold Lane. Treatment of the wounded was agreed between nations under the Geneva Convention drawn up in 1864, but in 1929, a second convention was drawn up for treatment of Prisoners of War. Japan signed but the Soviet Union did not. The Convention had no standing in international law, but the nations who signed it were morally obliged to conform to its principles. The prisoners were very useful in Norfolk. They were frequently used to work on the land.

A report to English Heritage from a farmer's daughter quotes:

"I used to collect three German prisoners of war and bring them to my parents' home to work on the farm. They worked well. When it was time for them to go back, one of them cried. I used to take them for breakfast in the morning and mother gave them a jug of tea and lunch. There was a Captain Richardson in charge of them, and he used to book them in and out each day. The prisoner of war camp used to be on the West side of the Heartsease Estate near Mousehold. They were used to clear mines from the beaches, but this was not strictly in accordance with the convention. In the harsh winter of 1947 they were used to clear snow from the roads. Local teams would play football against local prisoner of war teams, and prisoners of war would play against other local camps (remember Bert Trautmann who went on to play for Manchester City)."

The prisoners could watch films and even joined choirs. There were strict fraternisation rules but these were not always adhered to. As many as 796 women went on to marry German prisoners of war. As time went on the fraternisation rules were relaxed. The press and the radio reported that prisoners of war should be invited into British homes for Christmas and many did just that. By 1948 most had been repatriated, and in Norwich a farewell party was held at the Lads' Club for them organised by the Norwich International Fellowship Committee. Mr H Witard presided. One of the prisoners of war, Hans Dittrich, thanked the Norfolk and Norwich people for their hospitality, and said that in spite of the war, no one had ever showed any hostility towards them. Lt. Col J B Phillips, commandant of the camp, thanked the Fellowship Committee for making all the arrangements for the party. Hans Dittrich returned to his home town of Dresden, but he was still writing to Mrs Statham and her family in Norfolk, and exchanging presents and food parcels, especially at Christmas, as late as January 1950.

5 : VICTORY CELEBRATIONS

The end of the war led to celebrations, first in May 1945 to commemorate victory in Europe (VE Day) and then later in the year to mark victory in the Far East (VJ Day). As the photograph shows, street parties were held in Thorpe Hamlet as well as elsewhere.

Recognition of the contribution made to the war effort by those working in the Civil Service is shown in the following message sent by the Prime Minister, Winston Churchill on 8th May 1945 (and included in the next Post Office Circular).

On this historic day I wish to send to all those who have served the Crown as Civil Servants the thanks of His Majesty's Government.

This war which brought us to the brink of disaster called forth from the people of this country a response unsurpassed in our history. Behind the great achievements of the Nation now issuing in victory stands a proud record of determined endeavour and unflagging toil, knit together by sound organisation, and united in purpose.

In all this the Civil Service has played its part, unobtrusive and unspectacular maybe, but alert and indispensable, whilst bearing its full share of the hardships and strains of war.

To all is due a word of praise and commendation, to those who have served in depots, dockyards and offices in London, in the country, or abroad; to those who have chosen the Civil Service as their career, and to those who have joined the Government Service for the war, putting their special skill and experience at the disposal of the State. Men and women, young and old, all in the Service have given of their best in these tremendous years.

To-day we rejoice in the hour of victory. To-morrow we brace ourselves to the task before us of restoring and where need be rebuilding our dwellings and our life. In this task I know that the Civil Service, sterling in character and steady in purpose, will not be found wanting.

6 : COMMEMORATED IN THORPE HAMLET

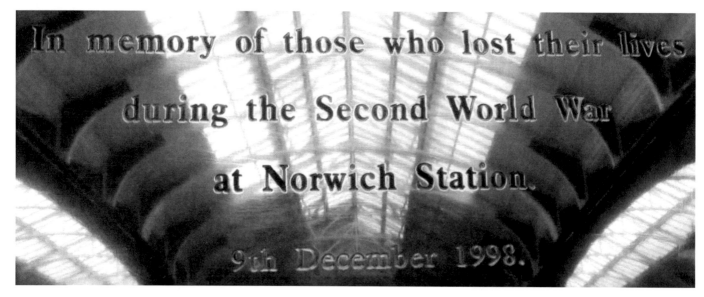

In memory of those who lost their lives

during the Second World War

at Norwich Station.

9th December 1998.

This chapter lists those whose death during the war is commemorated in Thorpe Hamlet. There are four locations for such commemoration:

- tombs and memorials in the Rosary Cemetery;

- a memorial sheet in St. Matthew's Church listing 10 military casualties and referring also to "the 23 civilian casualties from this parish";

- a tablet in the sorting office in Thorpe Road erected "in honour and remembrance of the following members of the Post Office staff in the Norwich Head Office area who gave their lives in the World War 1939-1945";

- Plaques at Thorpe railway station "In memory of those who lost their lives during the Second World War at Norwich station".

It is not unusual for a service man or woman to die in one place and be commemorated elsewhere. For example, Albert William Henden died as a prisoner of war in Thailand and was buried there, but is commemorated in the Rosary Cemetery. Many are commemorated by the Commonwealth War Graves Commission (CWG). It is not always easy to identify the details of those recorded in commemoration. The Group believes that the following details are accurate.

ERIC ALLEN Commemorated on the Post Office tablet, employed as Night Telephonist and Call Office Attendant. Served as Gunner 788960, 79 Field Regt., Royal Artillery died 10th October 1944. Also commemorated in the Jonkerbos Cemetery, Netherlands.

PETER ALLEN Commemorated on the Post Office tablet. Served as Sergeant Pilot 1333614, Royal Air Force Volunteer Reserve died 20th August 1942, aged 21 years when his plane (Oxford II AB 718) collided with another plane 4 miles SE of Grantham and crashed. Son of Samuel Walter and Gertrude Louisa Allen, of Lowestoft. Also commemorated in the Lowestoft (Kirkley) Cemetery, plot K/J/203.

Memorial tablet, Thorpe Road sorting office.

CHARLES HENRY BACON Commemorated in St. Matthew's Church as a civilian casualty. Died 9th July 1940, aged 36 years, when 40 Pilling Park Road was bombed.

WILLIAM GEORGE BALES Commemorated at Thorpe railway station as a civilian casualty. Died 1st August 1940, aged 32 years when the station was bombed.

IVOR HAMILTON BALLANCE Commemorated in the Rosary Cemetery, plot P2 &3/802. Served as Electrical Lieutenant, HMS Trinidad, Royal Naval Volunteer Reserve, died 29th March 1942, aged 30 years. Lieutenant Ballance died when HMS Trinidad was hit by one of its own torpedoes, and was buried at sea. The ship was part of an Arctic convoy. It is thought that the gyroscopic mechanism may have developed a fault because of the cold temperature. The ship did not sink, but was taken to Murmansk for repairs, and then set out on further convoy duties. She was later sunk that year on 15th May. Also commemorated on the CWG Plymouth Naval Memorial.

TRISTRAN GEORGE LANCE BALLANCE MC Commemorated in the Rosary Cemetery alongside his brother Ivor, plot P2 &3/802. Served as Major 73434, 16th Battalion, Durham Light Infantry, died 4th December 1943, aged 27 years. He was awarded the Military Cross for gallant and distinguished services during the Battle of Sedjenane. He took part in the Italian Campaign in late 1943, during which he died of wounds sustained in actions against the Winter Line near Monte Cassino in December 1943. He taught at Brighton College and played first-class cricket for Oxford University and minor counties cricket for Norfolk from 1932-39. Buried in the Minturno Cemetery, Italy.

CAROLINE MARY JANE BARKWAY Commemorated in St. Matthew's Church as a civilian casualty. Died 1st May 1942, a widow aged 89 years, when 143 Rosary Road (the Rosary Cemetery lodge) was bombed.

WILLIAM HERBERT HENRY BARRETT Commemorated on the Post Office tablet, employed as Postman. Served as Able Seaman D/SSX 12196, Royal Navy died 23rd November 1939, aged 31 years. Armed merchant cruiser H.M.S. Rawalpindi on Northern Patrol was sunk by the battlecruiser "Scharnhorst" as she and sister ship "Gneisenau" tried to break out into the Atlantic. Son of William and Agnes Barrett, of Norwich; husband of Ellen Barrett, of Norwich. Also commemorated on the Plymouth Naval Memorial.

GEORGE BEANE Commemorated in St. Matthew's Church. Served as Gunner, 14374647, 53 (Bolton) Field Regt., Royal Artillery died 12th May 1944, aged 34 years. Son of George and Harriet Beane; husband of Lillian Maude Beane, of Plumstead, Norfolk. He was recorded in the 1939 Register as living at 37 Wellesley Avenue and employed as builder's bricklayer. Also commemorated in the Cassino War Cemetery, Italy, and on the Bolton (Artillery) Memorial.

LEONARD PERCY BELL Commemorated at Thorpe railway station as a civilian casualty. Died 1st August 1940, aged 45 years when the station was bombed.

RAYMOND ALAN BERRY Commemorated in St. Matthew's Church. Served as Leading Aircraftman, 1332118, Royal Air Force Volunteer Reserve died 7th February 1942, aged 19 years. Son of John William and Beatrice May Berry, of Norwich. He was recorded in the 1939 Register as living at 72 Vincent Road and employed as flour mill labourer. Also commemorated in the Terrell (Oakland) Memorial Park, Texas, USA, which contains a plot of 20 Commonwealth burials of the Second World War, all airmen who died while training in Texas at the Basic Flying Training School (1 BFTS).

WILLIAM ALFRED BLAKE Commemorated in St. Matthew's Church, and in the Rosary cemetery, plot O1/969. Served as Private, 1574829, 1st Bn., Oxford and Bucks Light Infantry died 13th August 1944, aged 29 years. Son of William Andrew and Elizabeth Blake, of Norwich; husband of Dora Lily Blake, of Plumstead, Norwich. He was recorded in the 1939 Register as living at 73 Quebec Road and employed as railway engineers fitter's assistant. Also commemorated in the Banneville-La-Campagne War Cemetery, Normandy France. Most of the men buried there were killed in the fighting from the second week of July 1944, when Caen was captured, to the last week in August, when the Falaise Gap had been closed and the Allied forces were preparing their advance beyond the Seine.

LAURA BLOMFIELD Commemorated in St. Matthew's Church as a civilian casualty. Died 27th June 1942, a widow aged 84 years, when 16 Cotman Road was bombed.

OWEN CLIFFORD BRAZIER Commemorated on the Post Office tablet, employed as Postman. Served as Gunner 1764067, 113 Bty., 27 Lt. A.A. Regt., Royal Artillery, 7th December 1942, aged 32 years. Son of Herbert and Emily Brazier; husband of Ellen Maud Brazier, of Norwich. Also commemorated in the Benghazi War Cemetery, Libya.

DOROTHY BRIGHTON Commemorated in St. Matthew's Church as a civilian casualty and in the Rosary Cemetery, Plot O1/106. Died 30th April 1942, aged 32 years, when 16 Ethel Road was bombed.

HOWARD BRIGHTON Commemorated in St. Matthew's Church as a civilian casualty and in the Rosary Cemetery, Plot O1/106. Died 30th April 1942, aged 35 years, when 16 Ethel Road was bombed.

WILLIAM THOMAS BROOKS Commemorated in the Rosary Cemetery plot O3/903. Served as Colour Sergeant, CH/X 1950, Royal Marines died 16th July 1942, aged 54 years. Son of George and Helen Brooks; husband of Florence Elizabeth Brooks, of Norwich. Also served in the 1914-18 War.

KENNETH CARTER Commemorated in St. Matthew's Church as a military casualty, but it has not proved possible to identify him.

RUSSELL HARRY CROPP Commemorated in the Rosary Cemetery, Plot P1/926. Served as Private, 13047091, Pioneer Corps died 14th January 1942, aged 24 years. Son of Arthur and Kate R. Cropp, of Norwich; husband of Hetty L. Cropp, of Norwich.

EDWARD ROBERT CURTIS Commemorated in St. Matthew's Church. Served as Flying Officer Bomb Aimer, 128012, 10 Sqdn., Royal Air Force Volunteer Reserve died 28th May 1943, aged 18 years, when his plane (Halifax II JB960) was lost. Son of Alfred and Edith Curtis of Norwich, who were recorded in the 1939 Register as living at 32 Wellesley Avenue; husband of M. Curtis, of Rotherham, Yorkshire. Also commemorated in the Reichswald Forest War Cemetery, Germany, the largest Commonwealth cemetery in that country.

MARY ANN DAWSON Commemorated in the Rosary Cemetery, Plot O2&3/84. Civilian, died 28th April 1942, aged 63 years, killed by enemy action.

WILLIAM GEORGE DEBBAGE Commemorated at Thorpe railway station as a civilian casualty. Died 1st August 1940, aged 56 years when the station was bombed.

LEONARD CHARLES DYE Commemorated on the Post Office tablet. Served as Aircraftman 2nd Class, 961615, Royal Air Force Volunteer Reserve, died 31st October 1944, aged 24 years. Son of Herbert and Eliza Beatrice Dye, of Gorleston-on-Sea, Norfolk. Also commemorated in the Ambon War Cemetery, Indonesia.

CATHERINE EVE EDRICH Commemorated in St. Matthew's Church as a civilian casualty. Died 29th April 1942, a housewife aged 79 years, when 4 Hill House Road was bombed.

KENNETH GEORGE EWING Commemorated in the Rosary Cemetery, plot O3/1075. Served as Leading Aircraftman, 1250852, Royal Air Force Volunteer Reserve died 9th December 1946, aged 25 years. Son of Ernest George and Ethel Edith Ewing, of Norwich.

RAYMOND OLIVER FENTON Commemorated in the Rosary Cemetery, plot W1/1133. Served as Sergeant, 70226, Royal Air Force, died 25 September 1951, aged 31 years through war illness contracted overseas. Husband of Hazel and father of Susan.

JAMES OXENHAM FIELDING Commemorated in the Rosary Cemetery, Plot F/986. Served as Surgeon Lieutenant, HMS Hood, Royal Navy, died 24th May 1941, aged 30 years. Son of Dr. Saville James Fielding and Grace Fielding, of Norwich; husband of Dinth Grace Fielding. Cambridge University Athletics Blue. He had held the posts of clinical assistant in the ophthalmic, psychological medicine, and ear, nose, and throat departments, and senior ophthalmic house-surgeon, at St. Thomas's Hospital before entering the Royal Navy in 1938. Surgeon Lieutenant was on HMS Hood, when it was sunk by the Bismarck in the Batle of the Denmark Strait in the Atlantic. There were only three survivors out of the entire crew of 1418. Also commemorated on the Portsmouth Naval Memorial, Hampshire.

EDDIE FITZGERALD Commemorated in the Rosary Cemetery, Plot O3/302. Sergeant Wireless Operator/Air Gunner, 545600, 206 Sqdn., Royal Air Force died 14th August 1940, aged 21 years, when his plane (Lockheed Hudson I N7401) crashed five minutes after a night take-off at RAF Docking. Son of Edward and Mary Ann Fitzgerald, of Norwich.

CHARLES GEORGE FREEMAN Commemorated at Thorpe railway station as a civilian casualty. Died 9th July 1940, aged 44 years, when the station was bombed.

KENNETH TERENCE FULLER Commemorated in the Rosary Cemetery, Plot P1&2/758 Leading Aircraftman, Kenneth Terence Fuller, 1180216, B.S.R.U (Base Signals and Radar Unit), Royal Air Force Volunteer Reserve died 7th November 1944, aged 27 years. He died when a tank landing ship LST-420 carrying members of the BSRU to set up a new base in Belgium was hit by a mine near the Belgian coast. Son of Beatrice Alice Fuller, of Norwich. Also commemorated on the Runnymede Memorial, Surrey. The memorial commemorates more than 20,000 airmen and women who were lost in the Second World War during operations from bases in the United Kingdom and North and Western Europe who have no known grave.

WINIFRED MAY GAMBLE Commemorated in St. Matthew's Church as a civilian casualty and in the Rosary Cemetery, Plot O1/105. Died 30th April 1942, aged 36 years, when 58 Ella Road was bombed.

LILY AGNES GARROD Commemorated in the Rosary Cemetery, Plot A6/47. Died 29th April 1942, aged 47 years, killed by enemy action. Her husband George had been killed in World War I by enemy aircraft at Felixstowe in 1917.

CECIL EDWARD GARNER Commemorated in St. Matthew's Church. Served as Engine Room Artificer 4th Class, C/MX 72050, H.M. Submarine Unique, Royal Navy, died 10th October 1942, aged 23 years when his ship was lost. Son of Edward David and Ellen Elizabeth Garner, of Norwich. He was recorded in the 1939 Register as living at 63 Surrey Street, Norwich and employed as a maintenance fitter in a sheet metal shop. Also commemorated on the Chatham Naval Memorial, Kent.

PETER THOMAS GOODWIN Commemorated in St. Matthew's Church as a civilian casualty. Died 27th June 1942, aged 18 years, when the reception station at Britannia Barracks was bombed.

MAURICE IVAN FRANK GREEN Commemorated in the Rosary Cemetery, plot P1&2/693. Flying Officer Pilot Instructor, 86658, Royal Air Force Volunteer Reserve, died 27th February 1941, aged 26 years when his plane (Oxford R5957) crashed. Son of Frank and Dorothy Sarah Rose Green, of Norwich.

JACK GRICE Commemorated on the Post Office tablet. Served as Sergeant Wireless Operator/Air Gunner, 1870873, 12 (S.A.A.F.) Sqdn, Royal Air Force Volunteer Reserve died 31st August 1944. Jack Grice was a member of a bomber crew. On 31st August 1944 his aircraft (Martin B-26F-6-MA Marauder Mk II bomber) was on a flight from Pescara to Pesaro (north of Ancona) in Italy. The targets of the raid were tank traps and gun positions of the German defence line. In the target area another close aircraft exploded mid air and unfortunately the debris from this explosion brought down the aircraft of Jack Grice. Also commemorated in the Montecchio War Cemetery, Italy and on the Sheringham War Memorial.

Adjacent CWG memorials for Private Cropp and Corporal Gurney in the Rosary Cemetery.

GERALD CLAUDE GURNEY Commemorated in the Rosary Cemetery, Plot P2/926. Lance Corporal 2590863, 15th Div. Sigs., Royal Corps of Signals died 25th September 1941, aged 27 years. Son of Mr. and Mrs. Arthur William Gurney, of Norwich; husband of Rose Elizabeth Gurney, of Norwich.

BENJAMIN HAYHOE Commemorated in the Rosary Cemetery, Plot O3/104. Civilian, died 28th April 1942, aged 51 years, killed by enemy action.

JOSEPH GEORGE HAYLETT Commemorated in the Rosary Cemetery, Plot O1/87. Captain and Quartermaster, 202319, General List died 12th November 1943, aged 69 years. Son of Robert and Maria Haylett; husband of Ethel Josephine Haylett, of Norwich, and father of Josephine. In the 1939 Register he was recorded as living at 82 St Leonard's Road.

ALBERT WILLIAM HENDEN Commemorated in the Rosary Cemetery Plot O1/883. Served as Gunner, 980350, 88 Field Regt., Royal Artillery died 7th October 1943, aged 28 years whilst a prisoner of war in Thailand. Son of Oliver George and Alice May Henden, of Norwich; husband of Irene Mary Henden, of Lakenham, Norwich. Also commemorated in the Kanchanaburi War Cemetery, Thailand.

LYDIA MAY HEWITT Commemorated in St. Matthew's Church as a civilian casualty. Died 30th April 1942, a housewife aged 48 years, when 13 Ethel Road was bombed.

CHARLES JOSEPH HOPWOOD Commemorated at Thorpe railway station as a civilian casualty. Died 8th April 1941, aged 50 years, when the station was bombed.

BASIL JACK HOGG Commemorated in the Rosary Cemetery, Plot 1&2/623. Served as Flight Sergeant Pilot 1245813, 305 (Polish) Sqdn., Royal Air Force Volunteer Reserve died 24th September 1944, aged 24 years when his plane (Mosquito LR262) collided with another plane and crashed near RAF Lasham. Son of Alfred Charles and Mercy Catherine Hogg; husband of Maud Hogg, of Norwich. Recorded in the Post Office circulars as having worked for the Norwich Telephone Area, Skilled Workman Class II.

BERTIE HOULT Commemorated at Thorpe railway station as a civilian casualty and in the Rosary cemetery, plot O3/276. Lived at 12 Ethel Road. Died 9th July 1940, aged 55 years, when the station was bombed.

HERBERT ROBERT HOWES Commemorated at Thorpe railway station as a civilian casualty. Lived at 30 Ella Road. Died 1st August 1940, aged 47 years, when the station was bombed.

GORDON WILLIAM EGBERT JACOBS Commemorated in the Rosary Cemetery, Plot P2/843. Served as Corporal, 519291, 226 Sqdn., Royal Air Force. Died by accident on 31 May 1940 aged 24 years.

ERNEST RICHARD KEMP Commemorated in St. Matthew's Church as a civilian casualty. Died 31st May 1942, a fire watcher aged 61 years, when 6 Cedar Road was bombed.

FREDERICK JOHN KETT Commemorated in St. Matthew's Church as a civilian casualty. Died April 1942, a retired man aged 68 years, when 117 Ketts Hill was bombed

FREDERICK JAMES KIRK Commemorated on the Post Office tablet, employed as Allowance Deliverer at Gimingham. Served as Sapper 2003086, 221 Field Coy., Royal Engineers died 5th September 1944, aged 27 years. Son of Henry and Georgina Kirk, of Gimingham, Norfolk. Also commemorated in the Coriano Ridge War Cemetery, Italy. Coriano Ridge was the last important ridge in the way of the Allied advance in the Adriatic sector in the autumn of 1944.

STANLEY DOUGLAS LAFFLING Commemorated at Thorpe railway station as a civilian casualty. Died 9th July 1940, aged 23 years, when the station was bombed.

HETTY SELINA LESTER Commemorated in St. Matthew's Church as a civilian casualty. Died 27th June 1942, a spinster and domestic housekeeper aged 70 years, when 16 Cotman Road was bombed.

WILLIAM BENJAMIN LORD Commemorated at Thorpe railway station as a civilian casualty. Died 9th July 1940, aged 50 years, when the station was bombed.

GEORGE MANN Commemorated in St. Matthew's Church as a civilian casualty. Died 27th June 1942, aged 89 years, when 41 Spitalfields was bombed.

ALBERT EDWARD NELSON Commemorated on the Post Office tablet, employed as Postman, served as Gunner, 1070139, 31 Field Regt., Royal Artillery died 8th December 1943, aged 35 years. Also commemorated in the Ancona War Cemetery, Italy.

ERNEST JOSEPH PAGE Commemorated on the Post Office tablet, employed as Sorting Clerk and Telegraphist. Served as Trooper, 7932239, 3rd King's Own Hussars, Royal Armoured Corps, died 29th November 1943, aged 33 years. Son of William and Daisy Page; husband of E. Beulah P. Page, of Norwich. Also commemorated on the Singapore Memorial, which stands in Kranji War Cemetery. It bears the names of more than 24,000 casualties of the land and air forces of the Commonwealth who died during the campaigns in Malaya and Indonesia or in subsequent captivity and have no known grave.

ERNEST WILLIAM PALMER Commemorated in the Rosary Cemetery, Plot O 2&3/84. Civilian died 28th April 1942. Civilian, aged 65 years, killed by enemy action, also his daughter Betty Alexandra aged 24 years and grandchild Mary, aged 1 year.

RICHARD ALBERT PARKER Commemorated at Thorpe railway station as a civilian casualty and in the Rosary cemetery, plot O2/876. Lived at 5 Samuel Road. Died 9th July 1940, aged 23 years, when the station was bombed.

GEORGE ARTHUR PAYNE Commemorated at Thorpe railway station as a civilian casualty and in the Rosary cemetery, plot O1/888. Died 9th July 1940, aged 23 years, when the station was bombed.

WALTER HENRY PEROWNE Commemorated in the Rosary Cemetery, Plot D3/528. Leading Aircraftman 926871, Royal Air Force Volunteer Reserve died 20th August 1942, aged 30 years "whilst P O W in Far East" according to his memorial. Son of William James and Kate Perowne; husband of Betty Catherine Perowne, of Little Shelford, Cambridge. Also commemorated in the Jakarta War Cemetery, Indonesia.

EMILY POSTLE Commemorated in St. Matthew's Church as a civilian casualty. Died 1st May 1942, a widow aged 90 years, when 4 Hill House Road was bombed.

WALTER HENRY RADNEDGE Commemorated on the Post Office tablet, employed as Postman. Served as Leading Telegraphist, D/J 35143, H.M.S. Courageous, Royal Navy died 17th September 1939, aged 40 years. Fleet carrier 'Courageous' was sent to the bottom to the southwest of Ireland by submarine 'U-29' with heavy loss of life. Son of James and Beatrice Alice Radnedge; husband of Flora Radnedge, of Norwich. Also commemorated on the Plymouth Naval Memorial, which commemorates nearly 16,000 naval personnel of the Second World War who were lost or buried at sea.

GEORGE POINTER RAMSAY Commemorated in St. Matthew's Church. Served as Driver T/180745, 14 Gen. Transport Coy., Royal Army Service Corps died 14th November 1942 aged 25 years. Husband of Beatrice Ramsay, of Norwich. In the 1939 Register he was recorded as living at 68 St Williams Way, Thorpe St Andrew, and employed as wool merchant and fellmonger. Also commemorated on the Alamein Memorial, Egypt. The memorial commemorates nearly 12,000 servicemen of the British Empire who died in the Western Desert campaigns of the Second World War including the Battle of El Alamein.

CYRIL ROBERT RAVEN Commemorated in St. Matthew's Church as a civilian casualty and in the Rosary Cemetery, plot P3/942. Died 28th April 1942, master grocer aged 41 years, when the family shop at 49 St. Leonard's Road was bombed.

GLADYS PATRICIA RAVEN Commemorated in St. Matthew's Church as a civilian casualty and in the Rosary Cemetery, plot P3/942. Died 28th April 1942, stenographer aged 17 years, when the family shop at 49 St. Leonard's Road was bombed.

ZENA MARY RAVEN Commemorated in St. Matthew's Church as a civilian casualty and in the Rosary Cemetery, plot P3/942. Died 28th April 1942, scholar aged 15 years, when the family shop at 49 St. Leonard's Road was bombed.

WILLIAM JOHN RAYNER Commemorated in St. Matthew's Church. Served as Private, 14646673, 10th Bn., Highland Light Infantry (City of Glasgow Regiment), died 15th July 1944, aged 19 years. Son of William Alfred and Hilda Rose Rayner, of Norwich,

The Raven family memorial in the Rosary cemetery.

who were recorded in the 1939 Register as living at 49 Lion Wood Road. Also commemorated on the Bayuex Memorial, Normandy, France. The Memorial bears the names of more than 1,800 men of the Commonwealth land forces who died in the early stages of the Allied offensive in north-western Europe and have no known grave.

ERNEST JOHN SAYER Commemorated on the Post Office tablet, employed as Sorting Clerk and Telegraphist. Served as Aircraftman 2nd Class, 1290506, Royal Air Force Volunteer Reserve, died 16th October 1944, aged 33 years. Son of Albert Ernest and Lilian Sayer, of Beeston Common, Sheringham, Norfolk. Also commemorated in the Ambon War Cemetery, Indonesia.

THOMAS SCOTT Commemorated in St. Matthew's Church as a civilian casualty. Died 27th June 1942, a railway engine driver aged 50 years.

BENJAMIN SHRIMPLING Commemorated in St. Matthew's Church as a civilian casualty. Died 27th June 1942, aged 75 years, when 39 Spitalfields was bombed.

ERNEST ROBERT SILOM Commemorated at Thorpe railway station as a civilian casualty. Died 9th July 1940, aged 58 years, when the station was bombed.

EDITH MAY SMITH Commemorated in St. Matthew's Church as a civilian casualty. Died 27th June 1942, aged 30 years, when 4 Vincent Road was bombed.

EDWARD ALBERT SMITH Commemorated in the Rosary Cemetery, Plot O2/85. Served as Serjeant, 6340865, Corps of Military Police, died 25th April 1942, aged 28 years. Son of Edward John and Clara Rebecca Smith, of Norwich.

GRAHAM GOREHAM SMITH Commemorated in St. Matthew's Church as a civilian casualty. Died 27th June 1942, aged 6 months, when 4 Vincent Road was bombed.

HARRY GEORGE SMITH Commemorated in St. Matthew's Church as a civilian casualty. Died 27th June 1942, a motor engineer aged 34 years, when 4 Vincent Road was bombed.

MALCOLM GOREHAM SMITH Commemorated in St. Matthew's Church as a civilian casualty. Died 27th June 1942, aged 5 years, when 4 Vincent Road was bombed.

WALTER (WALLY) GEORGE SMITH Commemorated in the Rosary Cemetery, Plot O2/878. Civilian, died 9th July 1940, aged 23 years, killed by enemy action.

HENRY JOHN SNELLING Commemorated in the Rosary Cemetery, plot O3/900. Served as Pilot Officer Air Gunner, 109514, Royal Air Force Volunteer Reserve, died 25th April 1942, aged 26 years with the loss of his plane (Wellington Ic R1661). Son of Harry John Snelling, and of Ann Elizabeth Snelling, of Norwich.

JOHN LADBROOKE TADMAN Commemorated in the Rosary Cemetery, plot O2/1000. Died 11th July 1943, aged 35 years, killed by enemy action whilst a civilian on SS California. Son of John L. and Kate Tadman, of 111 St. Leonard's Road, Norwich. SS 'California' was a British ocean liner that was built in Glasgow in 1923 for Henderson Brothers and destroyed in the North Atlantic by a Luftwaffe air attack in 1943.

JOHN ROLAND SMITH WALLER Commemorated on the Post Office tablet, employed as Sorting Clerk and Telegraphist. Served as Sergeant Pilot, 1333615, 199 Sqdn., Royal Air Force Volunteer Reserve. He died aged 21 years lost in aircraft Wellington X HE634, which took off at 2300 on 27th May 1943 from Ingham, and was shot down by a night-fighter. Son of Cecil Clare and Katie Rebecca Waller; nephew of Lucy J. Grimley, of Norwich. Also commemorated in the Reichswald Forest War Cemetery, Germany, the largest Commonwealth cemetery in that country.

TERENCE LLOYD WASLEY Commemorated in the Rosary Cemetery, Plot P1/520. Private, 10th Norfolk Battalion, Home Guard died 15th June 1944, aged 33 years. Accidentally killed whilst on Home Guard Duty. "This kerbing is erected by Officers, NCO's and men of the 10th Norwich City Bn, Norfolk Home Guard to a gallant comrade."

STANLEY WILLIAM JAMES WATTS Commemorated on the Post Office tablet, employed as Postman. Served as Telegraphist, C/J 80287, H.M. Submarine Pandora, Royal Navy died 1st April 1942 when the submarine was lost. Son of Arthur and Emma Watts; husband of Florence Watts, of Norwich, Norfolk. Also commemorated on the Chatham Naval Memorial, Kent.

LESLIE ALBERT ROBERT WEAVERS Commemorated in St. Matthew's Church. Served as Boy 1st Class, C/JX 181915, H.M.S. Battleship Barham, Royal Navy died 25th November 1941. The ship began service in October 1915. She was present at the Battle of Jutland in May 1916 and after extensive service during WW2 was sunk by a U-Boat torpedo in the eastern Mediterranean. Also commemorated on the Chatham Naval Memorial, Kent.

ERNEST HAROLD WHYBROW Commemorated in St. Matthew's Church. Served as Sapper, 14592382, 3 Parachute Sqn., Royal Engineers died 10th June 1944, aged 19 years. Son of Charles Harold and Violet Whybrow, of Norwich. He was recorded in the 1939 Register as living at 62 Plumstead Road and employed as bay to pipe layer for telephone cables. Also commemorated in the Ranville War Cemetery, Normandy, France. Ranville was the first village to be liberated in France when the bridge over the Caen Canal was captured intact in the early hours of 6 June by troops of the 6th Airborne Division, who were landed nearby by parachute and glider.

ARTHUR WILBY Commemorated in the Rosary Cemetery, plot O2/106. Civilian, died 27th June 1942, aged 35 years, killed by enemy action. Husband of Kitty and brother of Nellie.

HELEN WRIGHT Commemorated in St. Matthew's Church as a civilian casualty. Died 29th April 1942, a housewife aged 78 years, when 1 Ella Road was bombed.

SOURCES AND FURTHER INFORMATION

Publications

Archant newspapers 17th/18th June 2016.

Frank Meeres, *Norfolk in the Second World War*, Phillimore, 2006.

Geoffrey Goreham, *Thorpe Hamlet,* The Thorpe Hamlet Association, 1972.

Joan Banger, *Norwich at War*, Poppyland Publishing, 2002.

Mary Ash (Editor), *Memories of Thorpe Hamlet, Norwich,* Memories of Thorpe Hamlet Project, 2004.

Neal Williams, *A Brief History of Cotman Road Norwich*, Lely, 1985.

Nicholas Webley (Editor), *A Taste of Wartime Britain,* Thorogood Publishing Ltd., 2003.

P E Hamlin (transcribed by), *Rosary Cemetery, Monumental Inscriptions 1819-1986 and Burials 1821-1837,* Norfolk Geneaology, Volume XVIII, Norfolk & Norwich Geneaological Society (now Norfolk Family History Society)

Peter Cooksley, *The Home Front, A Taste of Wartime Britain*, Thorogood Publishing Ltd., 2003.

Peter Cooksley, *The Home Front, Civilian Life in World War Two,* Tempus, 2007.

Post Office, *Circulars to Postmasters, 1939-1946,* consulted in the Discovery Room (Postal Archive) at the Postal Museum, London. The circulars contain rolls of honour for Post Office staff who lost their lives whilst serving with the Armed Forces.

Robert and Patricia Malcolmson, *Women at The Ready*, Little, Brown, 2013

Roger Smith, *The Canary Companion*, 5th edition, 2019.

Thorpe Hamlet History Group, *Shops in Thorpe Hamlet then and now*, Occasional Paper 2, 2nd edition 2016.

Websites

apps.eastsuffolk.gov.uk/pages/cemeteries/Kirkley/abbott_boggis.aspx [Kirkley cemetery]

bbc.co.uk/history/ww2peopleswar/

brightoncollegeremembers.com/roll-of-honour/tristan-balance

cwgc.org   [Commonwealth War Graves Commission]

digitalarchive.2ndair.org.uk [Digital archive of the Second Air Division of the United States Eighth Army Air Force (USAAF) - archive held at the Norfolk Record office.]

en.wikipedia.org/wiki/   Relevant articles incude: Air Raid Precautions in the United Kingdom; Civil Defence Service; National Registration Act 1939; Rationing in the United Kingdom; Royal Voluntary Service; Tristan Ballance

FindMyPast.co.uk   [Includes the 1939 Register, available on computers in Norfolk libraries]

friendsoftherosarycemetery.simdif.com

georgeplunkett.co.uk/Website/raids {George Plunkett's photographs of Norwich] heritage.norfolk.gov.uk [Norfolk Heritage Explorer Information can be accessed using the map facility [http://www.heritage.norfolk.gov.uk/map-search] or by entering the NHER (Norfolk Histroic Environment Record) number. Examples are 26456 (site of Home Guard Shelters in Lower Clarence Road) and 54262 (site of air raid shelters in the former football ground on Rosary Road).]

iwm.org.uk/memorials [The War Memorials Register, compiled by the Imperial War Museum]

maps.nls.uk/os [National Library of Scotland online access to old Ordnance Survey maps]

nationalarchives.gov.uk [The National Archives]

naval-history.net [Preserving naval history research and memoirs]

norfolk.gov.uk/libraries-local-history-and-archives/photo-collections/picture-norfolk Some of the items in the Picture Norfolk collection can be viewed online. For example, using "air raid shelters" in the search facility gives images of shelters in locations such as Chapelfield Gardens in Norwich.

postalmuseum.org [The Postal Museum]

rafcommands.com [Royal Air Force commands]

royalvoluntaryservice.org.uk/about-us/our-history

sheringhamrbl.co.uk/warmemorial/names/gricej.php [Sheringham Royal British Legion]

Organisations

Norfolk Heritage Centre (https://www.norfolk.gov.uk/libraries-local-history-and-archives/researching-family-and-local-history/norfolk-heritage-centre) Picture Norfolk folders for second world war.

Norfolk Record Office (archives.norfolk.gov.uk)

> We have particularly consulted the following files:
> N/EN 1 Air Raid Precaution Files
> N/EN 2 Civil Defence
> N/EN 3 Air Raid Shelter Site Plans
> N/EN 3/9 Maps of city showing ARP posts and gas, electricity and water systems
> Log books for Crome, Stuart and Thorpe Hamlet Schools

St. Matthew's Church, Thorpe Hamlet (stmatthewschurch.org.uk/)

Museums

Three of the museums in the Norfolk Museums Service have displays of objects referred to in this text. The **Museum of Norwich at the Bridewell** has extensive displays on air raids, including Wally's Map (made by 15-year old Wally Emms in 1942), evacuees and objects including Spitfire Cottage (made from cardboard and scraps during long hours on fire-watching duty and exhibited to raise money towards a Spitifre plane) and Mickey Mouse gas masks for the under-fives: "The bright colours were thought to make it look less scary than the adult version. Children soon discovered they could make rude noises by blowing out through the rubber."

Gressenhall Farm and Workhouse has a recreated Anderson shelter on the farm and displays in the Collections Gallery including a rather bizarre air

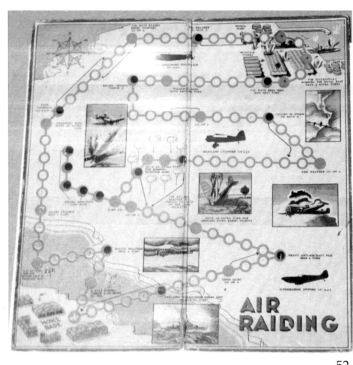

raid board game: "For successfully bombing the naval base have two extra turns"

In keeping with its rural emphasis the museum also has a display and mural on the work of the Women's Land Army.

Time and Tide Museum in Great Yarmouth has a Morrison shelter in the centre of a setting of a room in a house in the Rows in Great Yarmouth, where two ARP wardens lived - husband and wife who took it on turns to be on duty. The displays also include other items of equipment.

Women's Land Army mural at Gressenhall Farm and Workhouse.

Thorpe Hamlet in World War Two - the map opposite

The map opposite uses a modern base map of Thorpe Hamlet overlain with the following:

- Key targets for bombing raids in and close to Thorpe Hamlet - in blue;

- Locations where bombs were dropped - in red;

- Public air raid shelters - black circles;

- First aid posts - marked with 'A';

- School shelters open to the public outside school hours - marked with 'S' ;

- Air raid wardens posts - marked with 'W'

The base map uses Ordnance Survey Open Data Crown copyright and database right 2020. The shelter and warden information is taken from maps produced by the Norwich City Engineer and held in Norfolk Record Office N/EN 3/9 and N/EN 4/244. The bomb information is from the Norwich Bomb Map, available on a CD from Norfolk Record Office ACC 2007/195.

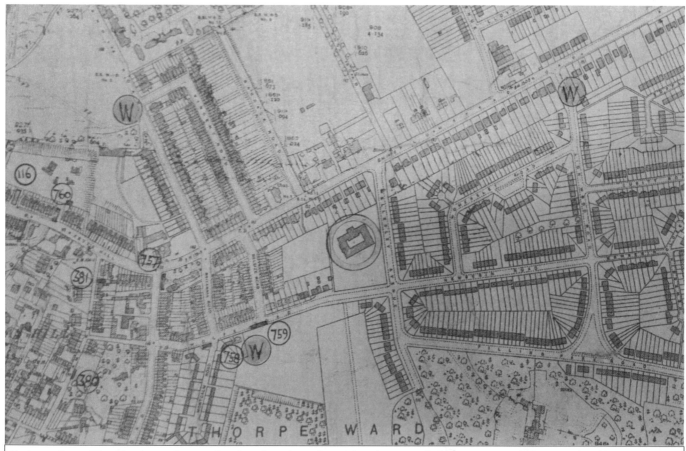

Extract from City Engineers' map showing location of wardens' posts, shelters, etc. Norfolk Record Office NRO N/ EN 3.